Myself and the World

Myself *and the* World

A BIOGRAPHY OF WILLIAM FAULKNER

Robert W. Hamblin

UNIVERSITY PRESS OF MISSISSIPPI ✦ JACKSON

Publication of this book was made possible in part
by a generous donation by the Center for Faulkner Studies
at Southeast Missouri State University.

www.upress.state.ms.us

The University Press of Mississippi is a member
of the Association of American University Presses.

First printing 2016

∞

Library of Congress Cataloging-in-Publication Data
Names: Hamblin, Robert W., author.
Title: Myself and the world : a biography of William Faulkner / Robert W.
Hamblin.
Description: Jackson : University Press of Mississippi, 2016. | Includes
bibliographical references and index.
Identifiers: LCCN 2015044558 (print) | LCCN 2016001781 (ebook) | ISBN
9781496805607 (hardback) | ISBN 9781496805614 (epub single) | ISBN
9781496805621 (epub institutional) | ISBN 9781496805638 (pdf single) |
ISBN 9781496805645 (pdf institutional)
Subjects: LCSH: Faulkner, William, 1897–1962. | Novelists, American—20th
century—Biography. | BISAC: JUVENILE NONFICTION / Biography &
Autobiography / Literary. | BIOGRAPHY & AUTOBIOGRAPHY / Literary.
Classification: LCC PS3511.A86 Z78435 2016 (print) | LCC PS3511.A86 (ebook) |
DDC 813/.52—dc23
LC record available at http://lccn.loc.gov/2015044558

British Library Cataloging-in-Publication Data available

To the memory of Louis Daniel Brodsky

Contents

Acknowledgments

———◦◦———

I WISH TO EXPRESS MY SINCEREST THANKS TO ANN ABADIE, who recommended me for this project to the University Press of Mississippi, and to Leila Salisbury, the director of the press, who invited me to write the book. Both have been extremely helpful at every stage of production.

My initial study and appreciation of Faulkner developed under the tutelage of two outstanding professors who were both noted Faulkner scholars: Thomas Daniel Young, in whose undergraduate Southern Literature class at Delta State University I first read Faulkner; and John Pilkington, my graduate advisor at the University of Mississippi. Dr. Pilkington directed both my master's thesis and doctoral dissertation on Faulkner, in the process becoming my mentor and friend for life.

My late dear friend of thirty-six years, Louis Daniel Brodsky, not only afforded me the unique opportunity to partner with him on numerous projects related to his marvelous collection of William Faulkner materials but also taught me more than I can ever say about generosity, loyalty, friendship, and (another mutual interest of ours) poetry.

I wish also to acknowledge my huge indebtedness to my Teaching Faulkner associates at the annual Faulkner and Yoknapatawpha conferences at the University of Mississippi: Jim Carothers, Charles Peek, Arlie Herron, Teresa Towner, and Terrell Tebbetts. One could not find more pleasant companions with whom to discuss and debate Faulkner.

Ann Abadie and Charles Peek read this book in manuscript and offered many useful comments and suggestions.

Over many years my university, Southeast Missouri State University, provided generous, ongoing support of my Faulkner research and teaching and also granted me the signal honor of serving as the founding director of its Center for Faulkner Studies.

My greatest debt of gratitude, as always, is to my wife Kaye, for her patience, understanding, encouragement, and love.

Preface

WILLIAM FAULKNER WANTED NO BIOGRAPHY. HE ONCE WROTE to Malcolm Cowley, the well-known literary critic, "It is my ambition to be, as a private individual, abolished and voided from history, leaving it markless, no refuse save the printed books. . . . It is my aim, and every effort bent, that the sum and history of my life, which in the same sentence is my obit and epitaph too, shall be them both: He made the books and he died."

Still, on another occasion he admitted to Cowley, "I am telling the same story over and over, which is myself and the world." At the University of Virginia, he told a group of students: "Any writer, to begin with, is writing his own biography because he has discovered the world and then suddenly discovered that the world is important enough or moving enough or tragic enough to put down on paper or in music or on canvas, and at that time all he knows is what has happened to him." In that same statement Faulkner went on to emphasize the crucial importance of the creative imagination in the growth and development of the artist, yet the biographical element remains the foundation on which the imagination builds.

Following the publication of a number of detailed biographies, beginning with Joseph Blotner's massive *Faulkner: A Biography* in 1974, we now know that Faulkner was among the most autobiographical of novelists. His poetry, fiction, and nonfiction are grounded in his own personal life and that of his family and region.

But it is not enough to examine the external facts and events of those lives and histories. There is also the inner Faulkner, the one he tried so hard (though ultimately without success) to hide from the world (and sometimes, it would appear, even from himself). As demonstrated by so many of Faulkner's experimentations in narrative viewpoint, there is *objective* reality but there is also *perceived* or *subjective* reality. And for Faulkner, as for his characters, both of these categories are of the utmost significance. In this little book I try to do justice to both Faulkners—the private as well as the public man.

Faulkner was right to insist that his books and not his life should be our principal concern. But the best preparation for reading those magnificent books is to have a good understanding of the life and experience—both outer and inner—from which they grew.

If this book leads readers to want to read (and reread) Faulkner's novels and stories, it will have served the purpose for which it is intended.

Myself and the World

ONE

Ancestor: The Old Colonel

"I WANT TO BE A WRITER LIKE MY GREAT-GRANDDADDY," BILLY Falkner told his third-grade classmates. Years later Billy's brother Jack was not surprised when he heard this story, believing that Billy had patterned his life in many ways after his famous ancestor, William Clark Falkner, who came to be known as "the Old Colonel."

That ancestor, who died eight years before Faulkner was born, had lived an adventurous, rags-to-riches life. Born in 1825 somewhere in Tennessee as his family migrated westward from the Carolinas, he spent at least some of his formative years in Ste. Genevieve, Missouri, where his parents settled for a time. However, around 1840 Falkner migrated to Pontotoc, Mississippi, to cast his lot with an uncle, T. J. Word, his mother's brother and a prominent north Mississippi lawyer. Census records from that period suggest that William's father, Joseph, had died, so perhaps the oldest son set out to seek support for his widowed mother and younger brothers and sisters.

A couple of years later, when William was seventeen, Word moved his law practice to Ripley, Mississippi, some forty miles north of Pontotoc, and his nephew accompanied him there. In Ripley, William worked for a time at the local jail, completed a rudimentary education, and began the study of law, first with Word and then, after Word moved on to Holly Springs, with another uncle, John Wesley Thompson.

Between 1847 and 1861 Falkner served briefly as a lieutenant during the Mexican War, established a family, practiced law, became a prominent landholder and slave owner, assumed an active role in

Colonel W. C. Falkner, 1889.

state politics, and wrote two books—an epic poem about the Mexican War entitled *The Siege of Monterey* and a romantic novel, *The Spanish Heroine*—neither of which enjoyed much success. During this period Falkner also became embroiled in a bizarre and controversial chain of violence that left two men dead by his hand and produced a legacy of hatred that would hound him for many years. In 1849 Robert Hindman, who had served with Falkner during the Mexican conflict, claimed that his election to membership in a fraternal organization had been blocked by Falkner. When Falkner denied the blackballing, Hindman called him a liar and pulled a revolver. In the struggle that ensued Falkner stabbed Hindman to death. Although a jury later exonerated Falkner of any wrongdoing, the bitterness of Hindman's family was not abated. Two years later, in February 1851, the Falkner-Hindman feud erupted again. During an argument with a Hindman sympathizer, Falkner drew a pistol and shot his adversary. Once again Falkner was indicted and brought to trial for murder; as before, however, he was acquitted.

As the Falkner-Hindman quarrel continued, the citizens of Ripley tended to side with one or the other of the principals. In 1857 one of Falkner's supporters attempted to kill Thomas Hindman Sr. Falkner intervened to thwart the attempt, but a few months later Hindman challenged Falkner to a duel. The terms called for the two men to meet in Arkansas, just across the river from Memphis. Only one witness, Matthew Galloway, editor of a Memphis newspaper, would be present. But the duel never took place, as Galloway somehow managed to convince Falkner and Hindman to forego their deadly encounter. Years later, Falkner expressed his gratitude to Galloway for this and other acts of friendship by dedicating *The White Rose of Memphis*, his most famous book, to him.

The problem with the Hindmans finally behind him, Falkner settled down in the late 1850s to practice law and expand his landholding interests. By the time of the outbreak of the Civil War he was one of the wealthiest and most influential men in north Mississippi.

Moreover, according to the 1860 census of Tippah County, his mother, Caroline, was now a member of his household; and his brother James had also become a practicing lawyer in the county.

When Mississippi seceded from the Union in 1861, Falkner helped raise a company of soldiers to support the cause of the Confederacy. Subsequently he was elected colonel of a regiment of infantry and thus secured the title he would carry for the rest of his life. Proving to be a valiant, if somewhat foolhardy soldier, Falkner was commended by General Pierre G. T. Beauregard for valor at Manassas Junction. By 1862, though, Falkner had fallen into disfavor with his troops and was voted out as commander. Some say Falkner's ouster was due to his harsh disciplinary measures; others say his troops thought his reckless conduct in battle unnecessarily endangered lives. In any event Falkner was replaced as colonel of the regiment. Disappointed but undaunted, he returned to Mississippi and, only three months later, reentered the fray as the leader of an irregular band of cavalry that he had organized. Between August 1862 and May 1863 Falkner led these troops in skirmishes with Union forces at various places in northern Mississippi and southern Tennessee. In October 1863, partly because of bad health and partly because of his failure to secure a promotion to the rank of general, Falkner resigned from the Confederate army. His activities for the remainder of the war remain mysterious. One report says that he rode with General Nathan Bedford Forrest during this period, while another account says that he spent these years dealing in contraband secured by running the Union blockades that encircled Memphis. The fact that after the war Falkner was able to recoup his property and fortune sooner than most defeated southerners suggests that the second account may be true.

One possible aspect of Falkner's life in Ripley, controversial now as then, was brought to light by historian Joel Williamson in his book *William Faulkner and Southern History*. Through close examination of the constitution of Colonel Falkner's household in the 1850s and '60s, as evidenced by the U.S. census records of those periods, Williamson provides strong if circumstantial evidence that Falkner fathered one or more biracial children by one of his female slaves, a woman named Emeline. Williamson located the grave of Emeline in the Ripley cemetery, only fifty yards from the Falkner family plot; and he traced the life and lineage of her daughter whose father may well have been

Page of Ripley Railroad ledger, in W. C. Falkner's hand.

Colonel Falkner: Fanny Forrest Falkner, named, Williamson specu-
lates, after Colonel Falkner's sister Frances and his favorite general,
Forrest. Fanny was graduated from Rust College, where, according
to local rumors, she was occasionally visited by Colonel Falkner;
and she married another Rust student, Matthew Dogan, eventually
moving with him to Marshall, Texas, where he became the longtime president of the famous black school Wiley College.

Following the Civil War, Falkner resumed his practice of law,
purchased additional properties, and then, in 1871, entered upon

Page of Ripley Railroad ledger, in R. J. Thurmond's hand.

a venture that would secure his reputation as an entrepreneur. The Mississippi legislature, in an attempt to speed reconstruction through the rebuilding of railroads, had voted to pay $4,000 per mile to any company that would build a railroad at least twenty-five miles in length. Shortly after this law was passed, a charter for the Ripley Railroad Company was issued to W. C. Falkner, R. J. Thurmond, and thirty-five other incorporators. The railroad, completed in 1872, extended north from Ripley to Middleton, Tennessee, where it intersected the Memphis and Charleston (South Carolina) road.

During the 1870s and '80s Colonel Falkner was actively involved in the difficult tasks of operating and expanding the railroad and of retaining control of the company. By 1888, the railroad had merged with other lines to become the Ship Island, Ripley, and Kentucky Railroad; the line had been extended southward through New Albany to Pontotoc; and plans were under way to link the road with a network of track reaching to the Gulf Coast.

In 1880 Colonel Falkner took time out from his various business enterprises to write a melodramatic novel titled (after the riverboat on which the action takes place) *The White Rose of Memphis*. Originally serialized in the local newspaper, the work proved so popular that a New York publisher issued the story in book form in 1881. The novel was an instant success, selling out the first printing of 8,000 copies within the first month. Eventually the book would be issued in thirty-six separate editions, the latest in 1953. Colonel Falkner subsequently wrote two additional books—*Rapid Ramblings in Europe*, in imitation of Mark Twain's *Innocents Abroad*, and *The Little Brick Church*, a novel—but his literary reputation is based almost solely on *The White Rose of Memphis*. It was probably family stories about the success of this book that prompted a young Billy Falkner to tell his third-grade class that he wanted to be a writer like his great-grandfather.

In 1889 Colonel Falkner stood for election to the Mississippi legislature, partly in the hope of influencing legislation to benefit his railroad. R. J. Thurmond, the former business partner now turned enemy, sided with one of Falkner's opponents in a bitter campaign. On November 5, after it had become apparent that Falkner had won his election bid, Thurmond assassinated Colonel Falkner on the public square in Ripley. Falkner was buried in the Ripley cemetery, in a grave still today marked by an eight-foot marble monument of himself that he had commissioned in New York just a few months before his death.

The details of W. C. Falkner's life and career, when transmuted by William Faulkner's imagination, would provide an abundance of material for the creation of the literary cosmos now known as Yoknapatawpha. The most obvious parallels are to be found in the similarities between Colonel Falkner and the fictional Colonel John Sartoris, a principal character in *Flags in the Dust*, *The Unvanquished*,

W. C. Falkner's statue in the Ripley cemetery.

and other narratives. Like his real-life model, Sartoris is a prominent landowner during the antebellum period and a daring Confederate colonel during the Civil War. After the war Sartoris builds a railroad and becomes involved in politics. He is eventually shot and killed by a former railroad partner named Redmond. Not surprisingly, certain facts about his great-grandfather are altered by Faulkner in his re-telling of the story. For example, Sartoris kills three men, not two, and two of his victims are carpetbaggers who threaten the traditional order of southern society. In addition, Sartoris is much more the conventional aristocrat than was his real-life counterpart, and the fictional death date is 1876, not 1889. Even with such alterations, however, readers cannot mistake the similarities between Colonel Sartoris and Colonel Falkner. In fact, no other character in all of Faulkner's work so closely resembles the actual prototype.

John Sartoris, however, represents, for the most part, something of an idealized portrait of Faulkner's great-grandfather. But surely Faulkner was aware of other aspects of Colonel Falkner's reputation as it was handed down in Ripley—his stubbornness, his arrogance, his harshness in his personal and business dealings, his proclivity to violence, and particularly his avaricious climb to wealth and social status. While he operated on a much smaller stage than, say, J. P. Morgan, John D. Rockefeller, John Jacob Astor, or Jay Gould, W. C. Falkner exemplifies the amoral social Darwinism that is characteristic of the robber barons of late nineteenth-century America. This aspect of the Old Colonel's career is perhaps better reflected in Faulkner's characterizations of Thomas Sutpen and Flem Snopes. Both Sutpen and Snopes, like the Old Colonel, are self-made, propertied men who let nothing—certainly not conscience or any concern for social or family responsibility—stand in the way of their material success.

If Joel Williamson is right in his suspicion that Colonel Falkner had a black "shadow family" in Ripley, and if William Faulkner suspected the same, then the Old Colonel might also have provided the model for the miscegenation of L. Q. C. McCaslin, the patriarch of the McCaslin clan in *Go Down, Moses*. Old McCaslin, as his grandson Ike discovers in reading the family ledgers kept by his father and uncle, had also fathered children by slave women. There is a tiny bit of textual evidence that Faulkner may have suspected that he had African American kinsmen. In the short story "There Was a Queen" the black servant Elnora is identified as the daughter of John Sartoris; and, as noted above, John Sartoris is the fictional counterpart of W. C. Falkner. In this connection it is tempting to view Ike McCaslin's attempts to locate and compensate his black kinsmen as a symbolic projection of William Faulkner's desire to offer reparations to his African American relatives through the creation of *Go Down, Moses*, Faulkner's most sympathetic handling of the race issue.

The manner in which the Old Colonel's story came down to Faulkner—in family stories told by his grandfather ("the Young Colonel"), his father, his great-aunt Alabama McLean (W. C. Falkner's daughter), and others—is also mirrored in Faulkner's fiction. One signature characteristic of Faulkner's novels is the narration of an event (past or present) from multiple perspectives. A good example of this technique is *Absalom, Absalom!*, in which the story of a man who has been dead for almost fifty years is retold by a number of narrators who employ personal recollection, second- and third-hand accounts, hearsay, rumor, and even guesswork to construct the story. The way Faulkner learned the story of his great-grandfather is very nearly an exact analog to the narrative method of *Absalom, Absalom!*

As Faulkner stated (with typical hyperbole), "I never read any history. I talked to people. . . . When I was a boy there were a lot of people around who had lived through it, and I would pick it up—I was just saturated with it." Since the Old Colonel had been such a controversial figure, the stories with which Faulkner was "saturated" were often contradictory. Faulkner told one biographer, "People at Ripley talk of him as if he were still alive, up in the hills some place, and might come in at any time. It's a strange thing; there are lots of people who knew him well, and yet no two of them remember him alike or describe him the same way. One will say he was like me [that is, small] and another will swear he was six feet tall."

W. C. Falkner was arguably the single greatest influence upon the fiction of William Faulkner. As noted, he is indisputably the prototype of John Sartoris and most likely, though to a lesser degree, a model as well for the characterizations of Thomas Sutpen, Flem Snopes, and L. Q. C. McCaslin. Moreover, the manner in which the story of Colonel Falkner came down to his great-grandson influenced Faulkner's understanding of the way history is transmitted from one generation to another, and that understanding in turn influenced the style and technique of Faulkner's novels. Finally, the contradictory events of Colonel Falkner's life and career provided Faulkner with an object lesson in the paradoxes of human nature. As we shall see later, much of Faulkner's writing turns on the contrast between an idealized versus a realistic view of the world. And the contradictory stories of the Old Colonel that were handed down to Faulkner convey both of these opposites.

Childhood and Adolescence

WILLIAM CUTHBERT FALKNER WAS BORN IN NEW ALBANY, Mississippi, on September 25, 1897. His father, Murry, was a third-generation worker for the family railroad; his mother, Maud, was a member of a prominent Oxford family, the Butlers. The baby was given the first name of his legendary great-grandfather and the middle name of his father.

For the first year of his life, young Billy suffered from colic, or excessive crying, a condition that afflicts a small percentage of infants. To give him relief, his mother would rock him in a straight-backed chair. Hearing the thumping of the chair on the wooden floor at all hours of the night, the neighbors thought the Falkners strange folks. "They chop kindlin' all night long," it was said.

Shortly after Billy's first birthday the family moved to Ripley, a small town twenty miles north of New Albany. Ripley had been the hometown of the Old Colonel, the place where the family railroad had gotten its start. Murry Falkner had received a promotion to auditor and treasurer for the railroad, and he was transferred to Ripley to carry out his new duties.

Shortly after the move to Ripley another son, Murry, nicknamed Jack, was added to the family; and then two years later, a third

Billy Falkner, aged eleven months.

son, John, was born. A few years later, after the family had moved to Oxford, a fourth boy, Dean, was born.

Billy continued to be a sickly and insecure child. When he was four he, as well as his brother Jack, almost died from a severe case of scarlet fever. His grandmother, Sallie Murry Falkner, came from Oxford to help Maud nurse the children through the illness.

On another occasion, when he was spending the night at the home of his great-aunt, Willie Medora Vance, Billy was overcome with what he remembered years later as "one of those spells of loneliness and nameless sorrow that children suffer" and had to be carried home in the middle of the night.

Billy Falkner, aged three.

The four years the family spent in Ripley may have been the happiest years of Murry Falkner's life. He loved the railroad, having dropped out of college to work on the road. Over the next few years he steadily moved up from fireman to engineer to conductor to stationmaster, and now to treasurer. He also acquired a farm outside town, where he enjoyed his horses and bird dogs.

But in 1902 that happy life in Ripley came to an abrupt halt. Murry's father, J. W. T. Falkner, "the Young Colonel," decided to sell the railroad. J. W. T., at the insistence of his wife, had left Ripley after the murder of his father, partly to avoid further trouble with Thurmond sympathizers. In Oxford he became a successful trial lawyer and also a prominent real estate owner, a state senator, a trustee of the University of Mississippi, and eventually a banker. Increasingly, the railroad became an unwanted burden, so he put it up for sale.

Murry was heartbroken. His father's offer to set him up in business in Oxford was small consolation. Murry frantically tried to borrow money to purchase the road from his father, but when that effort failed, and when his wife, Maud, nixed the idea of the family's migrating to Texas, he was left with no other option except to join his father in Oxford. Maud, however, was not at all unhappy about the move; she was pleased to be returning to her hometown.

Billy, Jack, and John, c. 1905.

For the young Falkner boys, the move to Oxford was an exciting event. Oxford was more than three times the size of Ripley, and there were many more things to see and do. Jack Falkner remembered the boys' first impression of Oxford: "We descended from the [railway] coach, and Bill and I were speechless with wonder; never had we seen so many people, so many horses and carriages, and so much movement everywhere."

Their new home had an adjacent pasture for stock, so Murry was able to keep his horses. From this beginning young Billy developed a love for horses and woods that would last his entire life.

Children from the neighborhood often joined the Falkner boys for games of baseball or football played in the large front yard, both at their home and at Grandfather's, called "the Big Place," located only a few blocks away. Billy taught the younger children how to play, often inventing his own rules for the games. His brother John would later recall how Billy created the games of "acorn baseball" and "horse baseball." In the former a base runner could be retired if another player threw an acorn and hit him with it. In the second game, the batter would hit the ball and then ride his horse around the bases. A problem developed, however, when Billy decided to combine the two games. Once, when Jack was riding his pony to first base, Billy cut loose with an acorn throw that hit the pony, causing him to bolt and run with Jack desperately clinging to the mane. After that incident both acorns and horses were banned from the boys' baseball games.

In addition to his mother, three other women came to be very influential on Billy's younger years. His mother's mother, Lelia Swift Butler, whom the family called "Damuddy," came to live in the home, remaining there until her death by cancer five years later; and a black woman, Caroline Barr, "Mammy Callie," was employed as a household servant. Damuddy took the children to church and, with Maud, directed their moral and religious training, while Mammy Callie told them stories and took them on hikes into the woods, where she named for them the different birds and flowers. She lived in a small house out back, but evenings, she sat with the family in her own rocking chair beside the fireplace, dipping snuff and sharing in the conversation.

The boys were also quite close with their "Auntee," Holland Wilkins, who had moved into the Big Place to care for her ailing mother and, after her mother's death, to manage the household for her father. Auntee was one of those indomitable, "unvanquished" women so prevalent in southern life and literature (including

Cousin Sallie Murry Wilkins with the Falkner boys, 1909

Faulkner's). As Jack Falkner remembered her, "We were of a common conviction that had Auntee lived at the time of the War, the South would never (could never) have lost it, seeing that the Yankee had us outnumbered by only three or four to one. Surely Auntee would have made up this trifling difference without half trying. . . . She knew nothing of the War first-hand, but she did live through the years that followed—the so-called Reconstruction period. I don't know what the carpetbaggers from the North reconstructed, but it wasn't Auntee." Auntee's daughter, Sallie Murry, became a constant companion, almost a sister, of the Falkner boys.

One of Billy's neighborhood playmates was Lida Estelle Oldham. One day when the Falkner boys came walking past her house, Estelle pointed to Billy and told her family's maid, "See that little boy. I'm going to marry him when I grow up."

Billy didn't start to school until he was eight years old, but he quickly became an honor pupil. In fact, he did so well in first grade that he was allowed to skip the second and enroll in third grade. He excelled in all subjects, but, encouraged by his mother and Damuddy, both of whom were artists, his principal interest was in drawing. One Sunday in church, before Damuddy saw what he was doing, he drew a picture of a locomotive in the hymnal.

Faulkner also became acutely interested in reading at an early age. His mother, a college graduate, introduced him to her favorite authors, including Shakespeare, Fielding, Poe, Dickens, Balzac, Conrad, and others. "It was Mother," Jack Falkner later recalled, "who gave us our love for literature—literature in any form that would entertain, broaden the mind, and make us aware of past history and present events." Billy also had access to his grandparents' voluminous library at the Big Place, which included numerous works of history as well as the novels of Dumas and Scott.

Growing up, the Falkner boys had freedom to roam the town—playing games with their friends, flying kites, shooting marbles, roller skating, waving at the trains that passed through town, and hanging around their father's livery stable, which used horses, wagons, and hacks to transport freight and passengers in Oxford. The boys also enjoyed going with their father on 'possum hunts and other outings in the Tallahatchie River bottom at the "Club House," a two-room cabin built by the Young Colonel and used by Murry Falkner and his friends.

Thus Billy Falkner, in his formative years, was immersed in two distinctly different lifestyles—the sedentary, artistic, literary life encouraged by his mother and the outdoor, manly, active life followed by his father. He enjoyed both worlds, but more and more, to the disappointment, and occasionally expressed contempt, of the father, young Billy found himself being drawn into the controlling sphere of his mother. Yet, throughout his life, in both actual and vicarious ways, he sought to prove to himself, and others, that he was the tough, masculine individual his father wanted him to be. At times, caught as he was between the opposing wills of his parents, the young boy must have experienced the feeling that the mature Faulkner attributed to one of his most compelling characters, Sarty Snopes of "Barn Burning"—"the terror and grief, the being pulled two ways like between two teams of horses."

The Falkner boys loved airplanes as much as they loved trains and horses. (All four of the Falkner brothers would eventually become licensed pilots.) Although they had never seen a plane, except for pictures in magazines, they decided one day to build their own. As the oldest boy, Billy directed the design and manufacture of the machine. Using strips of wood, baling wire, and wrapping paper, the boys, with Sallie Murry as an assistant and Mammy Callie as an interested spectator, assembled the plane and then dragged it to the edge of a huge ravine in the back pasture. Billy assured the others that the plane would fly like a kite, that all they had to do was push it over the edge of the ditch and watch it take flight. Once the contraption was positioned in place, teetering over the edge, Billy climbed into the pilot's seat and ordered the others to let go. As Jack Falkner later recalled the incident, the plane executed "a tail-first inverted loop," broke apart as it tumbled down the hill, and dumped its pilot into the bottom of the ditch. Although it was hard to tell in the chaos of the moment, the boys were convinced that Billy had become the first person in the state of Mississippi to be carried airborne.

One of the most memorable events of Faulkner's childhood, later depicted in one of John Faulkner's "Vanishing South" paintings, was the attempt of a hot-air balloonist to launch from an empty lot and soar above the stores and houses of Oxford. All day long citizens of the town, including the Falkner boys, watched the "balloonitic" and his assistant stoke the fire to fill the balloon with hot air. Finally, it was time for liftoff, and the pilot, blackened by the smoke from the coal oil fire and fortified in courage by the whiskey he had been drinking all day, laced on his parachute and tied himself to the balloon.

"Let her go, boys," the balloonist called to the volunteers holding the mooring ropes, and immediately the balloon began to ascend. Once aloft, however, it was caught in a heavy wind and began to careen erratically. The Falkner boys, seeing that it was headed in the direction of their home, ran to see where it would land. They arrived in their backyard just in time to see the balloon draped over the top of their chicken house and the pilot climbing out of the muck of their pig lot.

Another exciting event was the arrival, in 1908, of the first automobile in Oxford. It was a red Winton Six touring car that passed through town on its way to Memphis. The Falkner boys ran along the street behind it until it left town and disappeared from view.

The first Oxford citizen to own a car was John Buffaloe, who handmade his own car in his gun shop. The car actually ran, but it made so much noise it startled the horses on the town square. So Grandfather Falkner, a city alderman at the time, arranged to have a law passed prohibiting automobiles on the streets of Oxford. The law was never rescinded, but it was never enforced either, as more and more local citizens began to buy cars. Even Grandfather bought one, a 1909 Buick, and hired a black man, Chess Carothers, to chauffeur it for him. These are the car and driver that would be prominently featured a half century later in Faulkner's last novel, *The Reivers*.

The coming of the automobile, of course, meant the end of the livery stable business, in Oxford as elsewhere, so Murry Falkner had to change course once again. He bought a hardware store on the town square, which he operated for a few years until he became the business manager of the University of Mississippi. Nothing that he ever did, however, was as gratifying as his railroad work, and he seemed happy only when he was hunting in the woods or hanging out and drinking with his cronies. He read western novels, undoubtedly fantasizing about the free and adventurous life he could have led on a Texas ranch if only his wife had agreed to move there.

Increasingly, Billy became aware of the tension developing in his parents' marriage. Even the birth of Dean in 1907 failed to bring the couple closer together. Murry spent more and more time with his drinking and hunting buddies, and when he did come home, day or night, he seemed always to have the smell of liquor on his breath. When the drinking became excessive, Maud would drive him to a clinic in Memphis where he would be subjected to "the cure." But the treatments provided only temporary relief. All too soon, the drinking and the accompanying explosions of anger would resume.

While Oxford in most respects was a good town in which to grow up in the early years of the twentieth century, it was also a town in the heart of the Jim Crow South. In 1908, when Billy was eleven years old, Nelse Patton, a black man, was arrested for the alleged murder of a white woman and locked in the local jail. Before his trial, however, a mob led by a former United States senator overpowered the sheriff, killed Patton, and hung his mutilated body from a tree on the town square. The Falkners' home at that time was only a few blocks from the scene of the lynching, so it is highly unlikely that the young Billy didn't at least hear (or hear about) the commotion, even if he didn't witness any of the vigilante violence. The Patton lynching would later influence Faulkner's descriptions of the lynching of Joe Christmas in *Light in August* and of Will Mayes in "Dry September."

By the sixth grade, Billy exhibited more and more indifference toward school and also distanced himself from his feuding parents. Turning inward, he started playing hooky from school. At one point he was sent to Ripley to live with relatives in the hope that he could develop some self-discipline away from Oxford influences, but that strategy failed and he returned home. Friends of this period recall that he became less outgoing and active and was primarily interested in his drawing, reading, and, before long, writing. He began to exercise his imagination, making up stories that he told to others. One winter his mother noticed that Billy's chore of bringing in coal for the fireplace had been assigned to a neighborhood friend. She discovered that Billy was telling the friend stories, but was withholding the climax in order to entice the coal carrier to return the next day.

Jack, Billy, John, and Dean, c. 1910.

High school yearbook drawing by Faulkner, 1913.

High school yearbook drawing by Faulkner, 1913.

His creativity, as well as a developing sense of humor, also found expression in a series of pen-and-ink cartoons that he drew for a proposed Oxford Graded School yearbook that was never produced. These drawings include caricatures of the school principal, G. G. Hurst, and various faculty members, as well as cartoons that reflect an aversion (undoubtedly Faulkner's own) to school and homework. The most interesting of the cartoons is one showing Miss Ella Wright, the history teacher, turning the handle of a machine labeled "Demerit Mill" and grinding out punishment for a fierce, ogre-like "A. Lincoln." Drawn in miniature, at Lincoln's feet, and with his obvious approval, a large Union bully armed with a knife is attacking a small, unarmed Confederate. The caption on the drawing reads: "Them's my sentiments!" Almost certainly, those words, and the content of the drawing, reflect the Confederate bias in Miss Wright's teaching of history, but they probably mirror the young Billy Falkner's views as well.

By his mid-teens Faulkner had virtually quit school, though he would return briefly in September 1915 to play football. Though small in size, he was a capable quarterback and admired for his tough, gritty play. His only recorded gridiron heroic, however, was his tackle of a teammate who intercepted a pass and, in his confusion, started racing toward the wrong goal line. Billy succeeded in making a desperation tackle of his larger teammate, suffering a broken nose in the process.

As Faulkner moved from childhood into adolescence, he began to spend more time with Estelle Oldham. Soon they were constant companions. Estelle had not changed her mind about marrying that Falkner boy, and by now Billy felt the same way toward her. They took long walks together; they met at the local bookstore; they began to exchange poems they had written. They talked about someday getting married. Under Estelle's influence, Billy began to pay more attention to his appearance and dress, becoming something of a "dandy" in the eyes of his contemporaries. Estelle was beautiful, gregarious, and popular; and her young beau found in her acceptance and attention a confidence to offset his insecurities.

The two sweethearts were separated, however, in the fall of 1913, when Estelle left Oxford to enroll in Mary Baldwin College, a school for young women in Staunton, Virginia. Sixteen-year-old Billy Falkner was once more adrift and directionless, in need of something or someone to give purpose to his life. He would find both the following summer, in the person of Phil Stone.

THREE

Young Poet

IN THE SUMMER OF 1914 TWENTY-ONE-YEAR-OLD PHIL STONE
returned home to Oxford after a year of study at Yale University.
The son of a prominent lawyer who was also president of the Bank
of Oxford, Stone had already earned a bachelor's degree from the
University of Mississippi and now held a second bachelor's degree
from Yale. Although he would follow his father's wishes and enter
law school at Ole Miss in the fall in preparation for joining the family law firm, Stone's real love was literature; and at Yale he had been
introduced to the writings of such noted contemporary poets as T. S.
Eliot, Ezra Pound, Algernon Swinburne, and William Butler Yeats.

Stone was also an avid reader of a number
of influential avant-garde literary magazines,
including *Poetry* and the *Little Review*.

Back home in Oxford, Stone eagerly
shared his enthusiasm for literature, especially contemporary poetry, with a group of
young friends, including sixteen-year-old
Billy Falkner, who had just completed the
tenth grade. Impressed with some of Billy's
poems, Stone assumed the role of teacher and mentor to the young boy. Over the
next fifteen years Stone served as Faulkner's
principal guide into the world of literature
and the life of a writer. He shared with him

Billy Falkner, 1914. ideas he had brought home from Yale, he loaned the young writer books to read, and he read and critiqued Faulkner's poems. Many of their discussions took place as they took long walks in the woods surrounding Oxford. As Stone later recalled, "I gave him books to read—Swinburne, Keats and a number of the then moderns, such as Conrad Aiken and the Imagists in verse and Sherwood Anderson and the others in prose." So that his young protégé could learn something about the life of a practicing author, Stone occasionally took Faulkner to visit Stark Young, the successful Mississippi writer who lived in New York but often spent his summers in Oxford with his parents.

In "Verse Old and Nascent: A Pilgrimage," an essay written in 1924, Faulkner remembered his early interest in poetry partly as a means of impressing females of his acquaintanceship. The principal female of this group was Estelle Oldham, the childhood playmate and neighbor with whom Faulkner fell in love at an early age. The Falkners and Oldhams were close acquaintances, and Billy and Estelle were nearly inseparable in their teenage years. As they grew toward adulthood, it was generally accepted among their friends, and between the two of them, that someday they would be married.

But the obstacles to their love match proved too great to overcome. The Oldhams belonged to Oxford's aristocracy; the Falkners were a family in economic decline, Billy's father being the owner of a livery stable and Billy himself a high school dropout who seemed uninterested in finding a job, much less a career. His one attempt at regular employment, as a bookkeeper in his grandfather's bank, he found boring and unfulfilling, and he quit after only a few weeks. Later he said the only thing he learned from that job was "the medicinal value of [his grandfather's] liquor." He added, "Grandfather thought it was the janitor. Hard on the janitor."

When Cornell Franklin, a young lawyer from a wealthy Mississippi family, began to woo Estelle, now a student at Ole Miss, even she began to waver in her devotion to Billy. Still, she loved Billy; and when her parents pressured her into accepting Franklin's proposal of marriage, Estelle offered to elope with Billy. But Billy refused, unwilling to marry her without her father's consent. When Billy went to Major Oldham, however, to request permission to marry Estelle, the major exploded angrily. Billy had no job; he was living with his parents; how could he support a wife and family if he couldn't even support himself?

Faulkner as RAF cadet, 1918.

Estelle and Cornell Franklin were married on April 18, 1918. It was the same month Faulkner would later assign to the wedding of Caddy Compson and Herbert Head in *The Sound and the Fury*—another ill-fated marriage that broke a young man's heart.

In an attempt to assuage his grief over the loss of Estelle, Falkner determined to go to war. Fascinated by the fabulous deeds of the young aviators flying the newest weapon of warfare, the airplane, he decided to become a pilot. Too small be to be accepted into the American Air Force, he traveled to New

Drawings by Faulkner as RAF cadet, 1918.

York and enlisted as a cadet in the Canadian branch of the Royal Air Force. For the next five months *Faulkner* (the spelling of the family name he used when he enlisted and which he would use from this point forward) was engaged in pilot training in Toronto, but the war ended before he had even flown his first solo flight.

Returning home to Oxford, Faulkner adopted the pose of a returning war hero. He wore an RAF uniform about town, sporting wings he had likely purchased in a pawn shop. He walked with a limp from a training accident, supporting himself with a cane. He fabricated stories about being shot down over Germany and having a steel plate in his head from his war wounds. It would not be the last time in his life when he would exercise his imagination to create an inflated, heroic image of himself or to escape an unhappy reality.

Drawing by Faulkner in
Ole Miss yearbook.

As Faulkner moved into his early twenties, he still showed little interest in gainful employment. He lived with his parents in an upper room of a large house on the Ole Miss campus. He enrolled in English and French classes under a provision that waived college entrance requirements for veterans. He wrote reviews and poems for the student newspaper, *The Mississippian*, and drew illustrations for the college yearbook. He joined a drama group and wrote a play, titled "The Marionettes." He checked out books from the university library.

And all the while, with the continuing encouragement and tutelage of Phil Stone, he wrote poetry—lots of it. While the style of these poems is largely derivative, reflecting the influence of such poets as Swinburne, Housman, Eliot, and Aiken, there are distinctly personal elements as well—Faulkner's great love of the Mississippi landscape, his impressions of pilots and war, and, most crucially, his pain and regret over having lost the woman he loved to another man.

Illustrative of the poems of loss and unfulfillment is "L'Apres-Midi d'un Faune" ("The Afternoon of a Faun"), Faulkner's first piece of

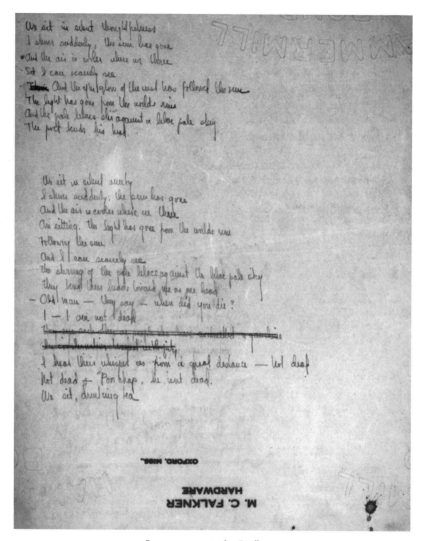

Poem manuscript by Faulkner.

writing to appear in a national publication—the August 6, 1919, issue of *The New Republic*. In this poem, modeled after one by the nineteenth-century French poet Stéphane Mallarmé, a faun longingly observes a group of beautiful nymphs frolicking in the woods. One nymph, in particular, claims his attention. He admires her "lascivious dreaming knees" and imagines the "hot extravagance / Of kisses on [his] limbs and neck." In his imagination he sees himself walking "hand in hand with her," but that reverie is shattered by the intrusion

Go tapping at the
With the minute ...
Then fall spreading ...
of the street
Into the s... once again.

There are whispering ...
of the dead
About her now, ~ wind th...
shadows
Of pale asphodels, and
wreathed abou...
While her song, ...
...
Still loops

Faulkner manuscript salvaged from ruins of Stone house.

of other "dancers, whirling past" and "a sound, like some great, deep bell stroke," that ends the dream.

In the course of the poem the narrator moves from being a mere voyeur to a wishful participant in the action, but ultimately he remains throughout the observer, the outsider fated never to be the participant. The final "bell stroke," symbolic of time, awakens the dreamer from his fantasy and returns him to actuality. Thus the poem introduces a dominant theme that will carry forward through the entire body of Faulkner's literary work: the conflict between life as desired and life as lived.

Years later Faulkner would have Bayard Sartoris, a major character in the novel *The Unvanquished*, say: "Those who can, do; those who cannot and suffer enough because they can't, write about it." In "L'Apres-Midi d'un Faune," as in so many of his early poems, Faulkner was learning how the act of writing enables one to bridge the gap between a romanticized ideal and harsh, disillusioning reality.

In these years when publishers were rejecting most of his submissions, Faulkner began a practice that he continued off and on throughout his career—the making of gift volumes of his writings for his friends and loved ones. He presented to Phil Stone a hand-lettered and hand-illustrated booklet of thirteen poems that he bound in red velvet cover and titled "The Lilacs." He prepared five hand-designed copies of his play "The Marionettes" which he distributed to his friends in the Ole Miss drama group. And, most revealingly, he presented a cycle of fourteen poems, titled "Vision in Spring," to Estelle Franklin on one of her visits back to Oxford following her marriage. In the title poem the narrator, hearing the ringing of bells at twilight, feels "A sudden vagueness of pain. That—he said, and trembled— / Was my heart, my ancient heart that broke." Later in the poem he ponders, "with his empty heart": "I had this thing I sought, that now has escaped me / When it was shattered apart." Clearly, Faulkner was still in love with his childhood sweetheart.

In the fall of 1921, at the encouragement of Stark Young, Faulkner traveled to New York, where he lived in Greenwich Village, worked briefly in a bookstore, continued his writing, and sought the acquaintanceship of other writers and critics. But still restless and unhappy, he returned to Oxford.

In December 1921 Faulkner began the longest tenure he would ever know at a full-time job other than writing—his three-year employment as postmaster at the University of Mississippi. Ironically, the position was secured for him by the very man who had objected to him as a son-in-law—Lemuel Oldham. The job would pay Faulkner $1,500 a year, not a paltry sum in those days.

Stories of Faulkner's days as postmaster are legion. Customers complained that he was slow in putting up the mail, and often misplaced it altogether, and he sometimes closed the window and retired to the back room to read or write—or even to go out for a round of golf. He read magazines and newspapers before he delivered them, and he frequently used the "Reading Room" for card games and parties with his friends. Eventually his dereliction of duty could no

longer be ignored, and in December 1924
an inspector wrote him a three-page letter,
detailing the complaints against him, including the charge that he was writing a book on
government time. Faulkner, who was ready
to quit the job anyway, told a friend: "I reckon I'll be at the beck and call of folks with
money all my life, but thank God I won't
ever again have to be at the beck and call of
every son of a bitch who's got two cents to
buy a stamp."

Around the same time, Faulkner was fired
from another job that he actually enjoyed:
that of volunteer scoutmaster of a local Boy
Scouts troop. By all accounts Faulkner was
an excellent scout leader, taking the boys on
nature hikes through the woods he loved
and introducing them to a game much like

William Faulkner, scoutmaster,
early 1920s.

modern-day orienteering. But a local minister, upon learning that
Faulkner was falling into the habit of drinking that had plagued his
father and grandfather, objected to Faulkner's working with young
boys. So Faulkner was relieved of his scouting duties.

During his time as a part-time student and postmaster on the
Ole Miss campus, Faulkner became fast friends with Ben Wasson,
a student from Greenville, Mississippi, who was greatly interested in
literature. Faulkner read poetry to Wasson, they drank moonshine
whiskey and listened to music together, and they both participated
in the drama group The Marionettes. Faulkner sometimes visited
Wasson's home in Greenville. At least one of his poems, "Pierrot,
Sitting Beside the Body of Colombine," was written there.

Faulkner's best friend in Oxford, however, remained Phil Stone,
who continued to encourage and promote Faulkner as a poet.
Faulkner accompanied Stone, an avid poker player, on his gambling
forays to Clarksdale in the Mississippi Delta and to Memphis; and
he often went on hunts with Stone and his father, General Stone, at
the Stones' hunting camp in the Big Woods northwest of Oxford.
But mostly the two men talked about literature, as Stone continued
to have unbounded faith in his protégé's writing future.

By 1924 Stone, feeling that Faulkner had enough quality poems to produce a book, sent a letter of inquiry to The Four Seas Company, a poetry press in Boston. The press expressed a willingness to consider the proposed volume, but only if the author or a sponsor could pay for the publication costs. Stone agreed to do so and asked Faulkner to assemble a manuscript from his numerous poems. Stone later claimed it was he who gave the manuscript its title, *The Marble Faun*, and he who mailed it to Four Seas. The volume, Faulkner's first published book, appeared on December 15, 1924.

The Marble Faun is a set of nineteen pastoral poems that contrast the active, vibrant life of the passing seasons with the statue of

Faulkner, 1924.

The Marble Faun, 1924.

a marble faun that is granted consciousness and sensitivity but is imprisoned in stone. The faun expresses sadness because he cannot break his "marble bonds" and enter into the lively scene around him. A "prisoner to dream," he longs to leave his pedestal and participate in actual experience. But his desire will never be fulfilled. "The whole world breathes and calls to me / Who marble-bound must ever be."

An age-old literary theme is the superiority of art, which is immortal, over life, which is temporal and fated for death. Faulkner would eventually come to identify with this notion himself, but at this early stage of his life and art, when he was still something of a disillusioned romantic, still hurting over the loss of Estelle and his disappointment in not

Promotional photo of Faulkner for *The Marble Faun*, 1924.

becoming a hero in battle, he had the marble-trapped faun lament that he will always be an observer, not a participant, thus never personally experiencing the happiness and joys of the living.

The marble faun, of course, is a projection of Faulkner's own feelings. Depressed and despondent, he confessed to Ben Wasson that he did not think he would live past thirty years of age. He even at some point during this period wrote his own epitaph, titled "Mississippi Hills: My Epitaph." In it he imagines himself dead and buried in the blue hills he loves, his only resurrection a natural one as his body decomposes to become food for the soil and the trees.

In many respects, despite a lifetime of trying, Faulkner would never succeed in escaping the melancholy that is captured so vividly in this and so many other of his youthful poems.

FOUR

Apprenticeship in Fiction

———⟞•⟝———

IN EARLY 1925 FAULKNER TRAVELED TO NEW ORLEANS, INTEND-
ing to stay there only long enough to book passage on a ship bound
for Europe. Having been unable to secure his reputation as a poet,
even with the recent publication of *The Marble Faun*, which had received mostly negative reviews, he decided to heed Phil Stone's advice
to emulate those writers like Robert Frost, Ernest Hemingway, and
Ezra Pound who had sought to advance their careers in Europe. But
it took Faulkner longer than he had anticipated to arrange his trip to
Europe, and by the time he did so, in July, he had added a new genre
to his writing portfolio—prose fiction.

In New Orleans Faulkner quickly became friends with Sherwood
Anderson, an established author whose collection of stories of
small-town life, *Winesburg, Ohio* (1919), was on its way to becoming
an American classic. Faulkner was introduced to the famous author
by Anderson's wife, Elizabeth Prall, who had managed the New
York bookstore in which Faulkner briefly worked in 1921. In New
Orleans Anderson complemented Stone as Faulkner's older friend
and mentor; as Faulkner later recalled, "We'd walk and he'd talk and
I'd listen, we'd meet in the evenings and we'd go to a drinking place
and we'd sit around till one or two o'clock drinking, and still me
listening to him talking."

One bit of advice Anderson gave Faulkner would eventually prove
to be prophetic. "You're a country boy; all you know is that little
patch up there in Mississippi where you started from," Anderson told
the young writer. Not until after he had written a novel about the

consequences of a war in which he never participated, and another about New Orleans dilettantes that he actually despised, did Faulkner heed Anderson's advice; but once he did so, he found his true métier in his native locale and the types of characters he knew best.

While Faulkner still thought of himself at this point primarily as a poet, he began, undoubtedly influenced by his conversations with Anderson, to experiment more and more with prose forms. He published a series of prose sketches in the *Times-Picayune*, the principal local newspaper, and in *The Double Dealer*, an up-and-coming literary magazine based in New Orleans. None of these sketches constitutes a fully developed short story, but they all exhibit characteristics that would become trademarks of Faulkner's successful fiction—a fascination for interesting character types, the use of action to illustrate a character's personality or psychology, technical virtuosity, and a keen eye for descriptive detail.

One of these sketches, "The Artist," undoubtedly expresses Faulkner's own personal ambition. "Where," his narrator asks, "is that flesh, what hand holds that blood to shape this dream within me in marble or sound, on canvas or paper, and live?" The sketch concludes: "But to create! Which among ye who have not this fire, can know this joy, let it be ever so fleet?"

During his first several days in New Orleans Faulkner boarded in a spare room in the Andersons' apartment, and Anderson later recalled how hard Faulkner worked at his writing. "I used to hear his typewriter rattling away as I went through the passageway," Anderson wrote. "I heard it in the morning, in the afternoon and often late at night. He was always at it, pounding away."

Back in Oxford, concerned that he had not heard from Faulkner for a while, Phil Stone telegraphed Faulkner: "WHATS THE MATTER DO YOU HAVE A MISTRESS." Faulkner answered: "YES AND SHES 30000 WORDS LONG." The book Faulkner was working on would be published a year later as his first novel, *Soldiers' Pay*. It would be dedicated to Sherwood Anderson, who had recommended it to his publisher, Boni and Liveright.

After Faulkner had worn out his welcome at the Andersons', he moved into an apartment on Pirates' Alley, a narrow street just off Jackson Square and next door to the grounds of the St. Louis Cathedral. His proximity to the cathedral provides just one example of how New Orleans presented to Faulkner new experiences that took him outside the culture and thought patterns in which he was raised—in this case, Old World Catholicism versus New World Puritanism. His subsequent travels to Europe, New York, Hollywood, and other places would further expand his sphere of influences.

Faulkner's neighbor in New Orleans was William Spratling, an artist who was also a professor of art and architecture at Tulane University. Spratling was well known for the lavish parties he hosted, characterized, in defiance of Prohibition, by the huge amounts of alcohol consumed by the guests. Faulkner proved to be quite the story at these parties—this quiet, little man who had a great capacity for drink and evoked immense sympathy with his tales of war-induced shell shock and the silver plate in his head.

At one of Spratling's parties Faulkner met Helen Baird. A twenty-one-year-old socialite from Nashville, she was spending the summer at her mother's vacation home in Pascagoula, just east of New Orleans. Faulkner was immediately attracted to her small, almost childlike appearance and her unconventional attitudes and behavior. Like him, she was also an artist, a sculptress. While Helen never developed a romantic interest in Faulkner, she found him fascinating and enjoyed spending time with him. They walked on the beach and

Helen Baird.

swam in the Gulf, went sailing, and sat on the back porch and talked. Faulkner even moved into the Stone family's cottage in Pascagoula so he could be closer to Helen and see her more often. He began to write poems for her, as he had for Estelle.

Also, as he had done for Estelle, Faulkner prepared a gift volume of poems addressed to his beloved. "Helen: A Courtship," written in Faulkner's fine, artistic script, contains fifteen sonnets. One describes her swimming. Others praise her physical attributes, including "the curving of her thighs" and her small breasts. Another poem imagines an interview of the prospective bridegroom with Helen's mother. All of the poems express a sincere and intense love that is not only physical but also spiritual: "he's quiet, being with her," one sonnet concludes.

Mostly what Faulkner did that spring and summer in New Orleans, however, was to write and complete his first novel, *Soldiers' Pay*, the story of Donald Mahon, a severely wounded World War I pilot who is returning home to die. Although the novel is set in the small southern town of Charlestown, Georgia, it is not so much a "southern" novel as it is an American, "Lost Generation" novel about the plight of wounded veterans returning to an insensitive homeland. Only two other veterans of the war—Joe Gilligan, a fellow soldier, and Margaret Powers, a nurse and war widow—show any real compassion for the dying Mahon. All the other characters, even Mahon's father, who is in denial of his son's condition, are wrapped up in their own selfish concerns and remain largely indifferent to Mahon's fate.

Faulkner finished *Soldiers' Pay* near the end of June 1925, mailed the manuscript to Boni and Liveright, and followed through on his much-delayed plan to travel to Europe. Accompanied by Spratling, he boarded a freighter headed to Genoa on July 7. The crossing took almost three weeks, much of which time Faulkner spent thinking and writing about Helen Baird. Upon arrival in Genoa, Spratling set out for Rome, while Faulkner headed for Rapallo, perhaps hoping to see Ezra Pound, who lived there. Apparently, though, Faulkner's shyness prevented him from trying to contact the famous poet.

Faulkner's letters to his mother detail his travels across Italy and Switzerland and eventually to Paris and London. In Pavia he admired the narrow, cobbled streets and the relaxed lifestyle of the villagers. In Milan the magnificent cathedral reminded him of "stone lace" or "frozen music." Stresa and Lake Maggiore were charming but too full of American tourists. He traveled by train through Switzerland, passing through Montreux and Geneva and viewing Mont Blanc, and arrived in Paris on August 13.

In Paris Faulkner and Spratling were reunited, but Spratling soon left to return to the United States, while Faulkner stayed on. He took an apartment near the Luxembourg Gardens, where he enjoyed watching children sailing their little boats on the pool and old men playing croquet. He visited all the tourist spots: the Eiffel Tower, the Louvre, the Arc de Triomphe, the Cathedral of Notre Dame, Versailles, the Bastille, and Montmartre. When he tired of

Faulkner in Paris, 1925.

Faulkner at Notre Dame Cathedral, Paris, 1925.

the city, he made outings into the countryside, to Tourain, Brittany, and other places.

The Luxembourg Gardens, with their broad avenues lined with huge chestnut trees, was clearly his favorite place in all of Paris. "I have come to think of the Luxembourg as my garden now," he wrote to his mother. "I sit and write there, and walk around to watch the children, and the croquet games. I always carry a piece of bread to feed the sparrows."

He visited the grave of Oscar Wilde and viewed James Joyce, whom he later described as "a genius who was electrocuted by the divine fire," sitting in an outdoor café. He grew a full beard, the one that appears in the famous photographs made of him by William Odiorne, an American photographer whom Faulkner had known in New Orleans, now living in Paris.

And, as he always did, wherever he was, Faulkner wrote. He was especially proud of one piece that has remained unidentified, writing to his mother: "I have just written such a beautiful thing that I am about to bust—2000 words about the Luxembourg gardens and death. It has a thin thread of plot, about a young woman, and it is poetry though written in prose form. I have worked on it for two whole days and every word is perfect."

Faulkner was still writing poems for Helen Baird, and now he started a novel based in part upon their relationship. Titled *Elmer*, it was never finished, but the fragment would be published after his death. The main character is a young artist, who, like the narrator of Faulkner's favorite poem, John Keats's "Ode on a Grecian Urn," is keenly conscious of mutability and death and thus admiring of lasting works of art that are "saying No to time." Faulkner had also started a novel about the artists and would-be artists he had met in New Orleans. This one would be finished the next year and published as *Mosquitoes*, his second novel.

In early October Faulkner left Paris to spend a week in England. He enjoyed seeing such famous sights as Buckingham Palace, Westminster Abbey, the Tower, and "all those old coffee houses where Ben Jonson and Addison and Marlowe sat and talked." But he didn't like the fog, which was "greasy" and "full of coal smoke," and he was saddened by the great number of beggars and unemployed young men that he saw. "They sell boxes of penny matches, play musical instruments, draw pictures on the pavement in colored chalk, steal—anything for a few coppers."

Much more amenable was the County of Kent, with its rolling hills, green meadows filled with sheep, and narrow, tree-bordered lanes. "Quietest most restful country under the sun," he wrote. "No wonder Joseph Conrad could write fine books here."

Nevertheless, finding England much more expensive than France, Faulkner cut short his visit and returned to Paris. As he prepared to leave London, he had a strange premonition. "I waked up yesterday with such a grand feeling that something out of the ordinary has happened to me that I am firmly expecting news of some sort—either very good or very bad."

It was good news. When he arrived in Paris, he learned that Boni and Liveright had accepted *Soldiers' Pay* for publication. Enclosed with the letter of notification was an advance royalty check for $200.

Eager to celebrate the publication of his first novel back home, Faulkner booked passage on a steamer headed to New York. Upon arrival there, he visited the offices of his new publisher and expressed his gratitude to one of the editors who voted to publish *Soldiers' Pay*. Then, to his great surprise, he bumped into Helen Baird, who was in New York trying to sell some of her artwork. Faulkner was ecstatic, but Helen responded to him in a cold and indifferent manner, disapproving of his beard and his unkempt appearance.

Disappointed in Helen's attitude, Faulkner took a train to Oxford, where he reunited with his family and awaited the appearance of his first novel. But he continued to obsess over Helen, despite her recent coldness toward him. Now expressing himself through prose, not poetry, he wrote an allegorical fable about a medieval knight's quest for the perfect love. Accompanied by two pages, Hunger and Pain, Sir Galwyn of Arthgyl travels in search of the ideal woman. In the course of his journey he meets three princesses, but each of them falls short of his vision. Finally, after being advised by Saint Francis that he will find perfection only in union with "Little Sister Death," Galwyn drowns himself in the stream of oblivion. Faulkner titled the story "Mayday," paradoxically alluding to both the season of rebirth and hope and the signal of distress that Faulkner knew from his military training.

Faulkner produced a hand-lettered version of the manuscript, added two pen-and-ink drawings for the endpapers, as well as three full-page watercolors to illustrate the text, and bound the small book in thin boards covered with mottled paper. He added a dedication to Helen: "to thee / O Wise and lovely / this: a fumbling in darkness."

However, by the time he presented the gift to her the following month, she was already engaged to Guy Lyman. For a second time, the woman that Faulkner madly loved would marry another man.

Soldiers' Pay was published on February 25, 1926, to generally favorable reviews. "An extraordinary performance," one reviewer noted;

Faulkner at work, Pascagoula, 1926.

"most noteworthy first novel of the year," another called it. The review that appeared in the *New York Times* noted the experimental design of the book and said it was written with "hard intelligence as well as consummate pity." In Faulkner's hometown, however, people held a different view. Faulkner's father refused to read the book, having been informed that some of the content was quite unsavory; and the Ole Miss library declined the offer of a free copy from Phil Stone.

After a short stay in Oxford and a side trip to Memphis to visit friends, Faulkner moved back to New Orleans, sharing an apartment with his friend Spratling. He was still desperately hoping to win Helen's love; additionally, he probably felt it useful to live in the city that was providing the setting and the characters of the novel he had begun in France and now planned to continue on site.

Faulkner in New Orleans, 1926.

One aspect of his life in New Orleans would be considerably altered this time there. Sherwood Anderson ceased to be his friend and mentor. Even though Anderson had recommended Faulkner to Boni and Liveright, he was developing a deep antagonism toward Faulkner. Some observers thought the breach was the result of pure artistic jealousy—Anderson was an older writer coping with the decline of his popularity and talent, while Faulkner was a young writer with seemingly unlimited potential. Others thought Anderson had been hurt by some unflattering comments Faulkner had made about him and his work in a newspaper essay. Then, too, there was the matter of their regional differences and loyalties: as a northerner, Anderson was very critical of the South, especially in the area of race relations, whereas Faulkner tended to react—and sometimes overreact—defensively when his native land was attacked. This argument had surfaced more than once in their conversations. Regardless of the reason, Faulkner and Anderson quit speaking to one another, and neither expressed any regret when Anderson left New Orleans in mid-1926 and moved to Virginia.

William Spratling's caricature of himself and Faulkner,
New Orleans, 1926.

Had Faulkner and Anderson not already been estranged, they likely would have become so after Faulkner teamed up with his friend Spratling to produce *Sherwood Anderson & Other Famous Creoles* in late 1926. For the small volume Spratling drew caricatures of forty-one individuals who were significant in the life of the French Quarter (one of the sketches poked fun at the authors themselves), and Faulkner added some of the captions and a foreword written in a parody of Anderson's style. Most of the subjects enjoyed the light satire and good humor of the work, but Anderson viewed the production as just one more betrayal by an ungrateful former friend.

Faulkner now turned his attention to *Mosquitoes*, which would be published in April 1927. The almost nonexistent plot of the novel turns on a four-day sailing party aboard a yacht on Lake Pontchartrain near

New Orleans. Members of the party include characters drawn from Faulkner's circle of French Quarter friends—a novelist, two poets, a sculptor, a painter, a critic, a matron of the arts, a businessman, a bootlegger, and a brother and sister pair who are much like Helen Baird and her brother Kenneth. The main event of the novel occurs with the accidental grounding of the yacht, which leads to the entire party's being victimized by huge mosquitoes. But this is not an action story; it is a novel of ideas. "Talk, talk, talk," complains one of the characters (and most readers); but it is the talk that represents the considerable merit that the novel possesses.

Looking back on *Mosquitoes* from the advantage of Faulkner's future achievements, one can see that in this second novel he is exploring ideas about life, art, characters, and techniques that he would employ one way or another throughout the remainder of his career. The best way to approach this novel is to imagine one is reading a transcript of a seminar in creative writing. A look at only a few of the major quotations from the book will demonstrate the issues Faulkner was contemplating.

"Genius. A hard taskmaster, isn't it? . . . It is a long lonely road."

"In life, anything might happen; in actual life people will do anything. It's only in books that people must function according to arbitrary rules of conduct and probability."

"And there's the seat of your bewilderment, Dawson—your belief that the function of creating art depends on geography."

"All poets in their hearts consider prosewriters shirkers, don't they?"

"I don't claim that words have life in themselves. But words brought into a happy conjunction produce something that lives. . . ."

"Human nature don't change. Its actions achieve different results under different conditions, but human nature don't change."

"You don't commit suicide when you are disappointed in love. You write a book."

"What is there worth the effort and despair of writing about, except love and death?"

"All artists are kind of insane. Don't you think so?"

"The poetry of modern poets is like a pair of shoes that only those whose feet are shaped like the cobbler's feet, can wear; while the old boys turned out shoes that anybody who can walk at all can wear."

"A book is the writer's secret life, the dark twin of a man."

"Art reminds us of our youth, of that age when life don't need to have her face lifted every so often for you to consider her beautiful."

"In art, a man can create without any assistance at all: what he does is his. A perversion, I grant you, but a perversion that builds Chartres and invents Lear is a pretty good thing."

"Dante invented Beatrice, creating himself a maid that life had not had time to create, and laid upon her frail and unbowed shoulders the whole burden of man's history of his impossible heart's desire."

"[Art] is that Passion Week of the heart, that instant of timeless beatitude . . .—that passive state of the heart with which the mind, the brain, has nothing to do at all, in which the hackneyed accidents which make up this world—love and life and death and sex and sorrow—brought together by chance in perfect proportions, take on a kind of splendid and timeless beauty."

Since, taken as a whole, *Mosquitoes* is a satirical attack on would-be artists, those who talk a lot about art but never produce it (Gordon the sculptor being the only genuine artist in the book), many of the statements like those above seem intended sarcastically or even cynically. But some undoubtedly reflect Faulkner's actual feelings, and all of them (and the many other similar comments in the book) contribute to the serious self-dialogue that Faulkner engaged in as he moved from poetry to prose and contemplated the shape and substance of his future books.

No one should read *Mosquitoes* looking for a good story. But everyone interested in Faulkner's growth and development as an artist should read it. Faulkner's second novel is a rich vein of ore from which he mined great treasures in the years to come.

FIVE

Creation of Yoknapatawpha

———⬥———

IN LATE 1926 AND EARLY 1927, HEEDING SHERWOOD ANDERSON'S advice to write about "that little patch up there in Mississippi," Faulkner began the series of stories and novels that would become his Yoknapatawpha chronicle. Almost simultaneously two narratives from opposite ends of the socioeconomic spectrum grabbed hold of his imagination.

The first, born of the tall tales he had heard from Phil Stone about the rise of the rednecks, was the story of the Snopeses, an amoral, poor-white clan that was displacing the old aristocratic order. In the first of his numerous ironical reversals of biblical narratives, this one the story of the Old Testament Hebrews' quest for the Promised Land, these rapacious descendants of a "Father Abraham" were multiplying and swarming across the entire county, devouring everything and everyone in their path. The principal member of the bunch, Flem Snopes, used all manner of unscrupulous means to rise to the presidency of a bank in Jefferson.

The other narrative, originally conceived as *Flags in the Dust*, focused on the decline of one of those aristocratic families, the Sartorises, modeled in large measure on Faulkner's own family. Its patriarch, John Sartoris, had, like W. C. Falkner, served as a colonel in the Civil War, built a railroad, and died at the hand of a former business partner. His son was the president of another bank in Jefferson, and his twin grandsons were both airplane pilots in World War I. Interwoven into the Sartoris narrative are numerous poor

Oxford, c. 1927.

whites, yeoman farmers, and African Americans of the type Faulkner daily saw in Oxford and the surrounding countryside.

Years later, looking back and reflecting on the genesis of his fictional Yoknapatawpha, Faulkner observed: "I discovered that my own little postage stamp of native soil was worth writing about and that I would never live long enough to exhaust it, and that by sublimating the actual into apocryphal I would have complete liberty to use whatever talent I might have to its absolute top. It opened up a gold mine of other peoples." Sherwood Anderson had been right, and Faulkner was wise to follow the older writer's advice.

Faulkner came home for Christmas 1926 and decided to stay on in Oxford, moving back into the attic room in his parents' house on the university campus. Perhaps New Orleans was not as appealing to him, now that Helen Baird was married. Or perhaps it was because another woman of his close acquaintance had also returned to Oxford. With her two children—Victoria ("Cho-Cho") and Malcolm—Estelle Oldham Franklin, separated from her husband and awaiting their divorce decree, was living in her parents' home. Immediately, she and Faulkner started seeing each other again.

Dissatisfied with the amorphous structure of "Father Abraham," Faulkner laid that manuscript aside for the time being and devoted his full attention to *Flags in the Dust*. He peopled the novel with characters he knew well. In addition to reprising the career of his great-grandfather, he drew upon Grandfather J. W. T. Falkner for his portrayal of Bayard Sartoris and upon Auntee Holland for the characterization of Aunt Jenny Du Pre. A Faulkner family retainer, Ned Barnett, provided character traits for Simon Strother; and both Phil Stone and Ben Wasson saw something of themselves in the characterization of Horace Benbow. The reckless driving habits of Faulkner's brother Jack paralleled those of young Bayard Sartoris. Faulkner's self-characterization may have found its way into the novel in the aesthetic tastes of Benbow, the Sartoris brothers' love of airplanes, and the fatalism of young Bayard.

Estelle Oldham Franklin, Shanghai, 1920s.

Ultimately *Flags in the Dust* is a story of decline, loss, and grief. Spanning four generations of the Sartoris family, the novel moves from the heroic exploits of Colonel John Sartoris during the Civil War and Reconstruction, through the life and career of his son Bayard in the late nineteenth and early twentieth centuries, on through the self-destructive actions of the twin brothers John and young Bayard during World War I and afterward, to the birth of young Bayard's son, Benbow. The overarching theme of the book is expressed by the omniscient narrator, in the observation that the Sartorises represent "a game outmoded and played with pawns shaped too late and to an old dead pattern. . . . For there is death in the sound of it, and a glamorous fatality, like silver pennons downrushing at sunset, or a dying fall of horns along the road to Ronceveaux."

Living again in his parents' home gave Faulkner the opportunity to bond with his younger brother Dean. An outdoorsman like his father, an outstanding athlete, and a friendly, charismatic person, Dean was the most popular and engaging of all the Falkner boys. Like his oldest brother, Dean was interested in drawing and writing, and William provided him instructions in both. Faulkner seemed to relish his paternal role with Dean, perhaps motivated in part by a keen reminder of the absence of a close relationship he had experienced with his father.

Faulkner resumed his courtship of Estelle. He wrote a children's story, "The Wishing Tree," and produced a handmade copy that he presented to Cho-Cho on her eighth birthday. The book was a gift of courtship to Cho-Cho's mother as much as a present to the young child. In fact, Faulkner was spending so much time at the Oldhams' that he was being referred to around town as "Major Oldham's yard boy."

Faulkner's writing of *Flags in the Dust* advanced rapidly; he had clearly found his subject and focus in the rich materials of his native locale. Just as importantly, he had discovered what would become a signature trademark of his later fiction: the interrelationship of the present with the past. When he finished the manuscript he rushed it off to the publisher, with a letter that reflected the pride he had in the work: "At last and certainly . . . I have written THE book, of which those other things were but foals. I believe it is the damdest best book you'll look at this year, and any other publisher."

But the news that came back from the publisher was devastating. Boni and Liveright rejected the book, concluding that the plot was too disorganized and the character development too weak. "The story really doesn't get anywhere and has a thousand loose ends," Liveright wrote, adding that even heavy revision would not likely make the book any better.

Faulkner responded in disbelief and anger, feeling "like a parent who is told that its child is a thief or an idiot or a leper." He expressed his frustration in a letter to Liveright: "I have a belly full of writing, now, since you folks in the publishing business claim that a book like that last one I sent you is blah. I think now that I'll sell my typewriter and go to work—though God knows, it's sacrilege to waste that talent for idleness which I possess." Faulkner asked Liveright to return the manuscript so he could perhaps place it with another publisher.

Even as he was deciding what to do with *Flags in the Dust*, Faulkner had already started his next novel. This one he would write for himself, not for the unpredictable whim of publishers. As he remembered years later, "One day I seemed to shut a door between me and all publishers' addresses and book lists. I said to myself, Now

I can write. Now I can make myself a vase like that which the old Roman kept at his bedside and wore the rim slowly away with kissing it." Like many of his novels and stories, Faulkner said, this one began with a single image: that of a little girl climbing a tree and of her brothers looking up at the muddy seat of her panties. The little girl was Caddy Compson, whom Faulkner ever after would call his "heart's darling."

The Sound and the Fury, as the novel came to be titled, was like nothing that had previously appeared in American, or even world, literature. It tells the story of the Compson family's disintegration from four different perspectives—the viewpoints of three brothers and a final omnisciently narrated chapter ("the Dilsey section") that counterbalances the subjectivity of the previous chapters. The main character is the sister, Caddy, and although she is not assigned her own first-person narrative, it is she who controls the entire novel.

The first three sections of the novel are presented, successively, by the three Compson brothers: Benjy, the thirty-three-year-old man with the mind of a child; Quentin, the troubled college student who commits suicide; and Jason, the selfish and ruthless materialist. All of these sections employ stream-of-consciousness technique, but each one is brilliantly adapted to the intelligence, outlook, and emotional state of the respective narrator. The fourth section discards the private and personal viewpoint to relate the story in an objective, third-person narration. Thus the movement of the novel is from the inner to the outer, from the personal to the objective, from the self to the world.

The overall structure of the novel is symphonic in nature. Just as a symphony moves from section to section, presenting varying moods and impressions, alternating speeds and rhythms, at times introducing leitmotifs and themes that will be developed more fully later on, at other times looping backward to recapitulate earlier themes, but always advancing toward a final resolution, so too does *The Sound and the Fury* employ shifting tones and impressions, hints and foreshadowings, repetitions and recapitulations, and time shifts looping backward and forward, all consciously designed to shape the story not so much on the pages of the book but in the reader's mind and imagination. There has been nothing quite like this book, before or since, especially the Benjy section in which Faulkner convincingly portrays the mental processes of a mentally challenged individual.

Benjy Compson's fence.

Even though Boni and Liveright had rejected *Flags in the Dust*,
Faulkner had not given up on that book. When the firm finally gave
him permission to shop it around to other publishers, Faulkner sent
the manuscript to his friend Ben Wasson, now a literary agent in
New York. Wasson recommended the book to a number of editors,
including Harrison Smith of Harcourt, Brace & Company. Smith
liked the book and persuaded Alfred Harcourt to accept the manuscript for publication, but Harcourt's acceptance was conditional
upon the book's content being cut by at least a quarter. Skeptical of
Faulkner's willingness or ability to perform such a task, Harcourt
asked Wasson to do the revision.

Faulkner accepted Wasson's offer to cut the manuscript and traveled to New York to be available to assist as needed. He took with
him the manuscript of *The Sound and the Fury*, which at this point
was nearly finished. Although he had expressed the belief that no publisher would ever accept such an experimental text, Harcourt's acceptance of *Sartoris* (the revised title for the condensed *Flags in the Dust*)

had lighted a glimmer of hope that the firm might publish *The Sound and the Fury* as well. Having Wasson and Smith in his corner bolstered his hopes.

In New York, as Wasson labored on the revision of *Flags in the Dust,* Faulkner completed the draft of *The Sound and the Fury.* One day in October 1928, in Wasson's apartment, he tossed the typescript of the new novel onto the bed and said, "Read this, Bud. It's a real son of a bitch."

Faulkner spent almost three months in New York, assisting Wasson with the revision of *Flags in the Dust,* completing and advertising *The Sound and the Fury,* and unsuccessfully offering a number of short stories to various publications. As expect-

Ben Wasson.

ed, Harcourt declined to publish *The Sound and the Fury,* but Hal Smith, who was preparing to leave Harcourt to become a partner in a new publishing firm, indicated a possible interest in publishing it.

Back home in Oxford, as Faulkner awaited the January 1929 publication of *Sartoris,* completed the final revisions of *The Sound and the Fury,* and contemplated his next novel, complications developed in his relationship with Estelle. By now they may have become lovers, but he had discovered that she had come home to Oxford as a very sick woman, distraught over her failed marriage and the drawn-out divorce proceedings, anxious about her and her children's future, addicted to alcohol, and dangerously close to a nervous breakdown. He still loved her, but could he ever completely forgive her for marrying Franklin? Moreover, his financial situation was no better now than it had been when he lost Estelle a decade earlier. In fact, Lem Oldham let him know that he was still unacceptable as a son-in-law. Estelle's sister Dot, however, was of another opinion, pressuring Faulkner to marry Estelle to quell the local scandal that was brewing about the couple's intimacy.

Psychoanalysts might be tempted to find something of Faulkner's ambivalence toward Estelle (and even a subconscious revenge) in the characterization of Temple Drake in the novel he was currently working on, *Sanctuary*. An Ole Miss coquette as Estelle Oldham had been, Temple is raped with a corncob by an impotent Memphis gangster, and then kidnapped and forced into a life of prostitution in a Memphis brothel. As shocking as those details are, the reader is more shocked to learn that Temple actually enjoys her life in the brothel and the Memphis underworld.

Faulkner later explained that he intended *Sanctuary* to be a shocker. Upset that a great book like *The Sound and the Fury* had found few advocates, he said he vowed to create "the most horrific tale [he] could imagine," confident that a book about rape, incest, and multiple murders would be quite popular with the sensation-hungry public. However, when he sent the typescript to Harrison Smith, the publisher wrote back, "Good God, I can't publish this. We'd both be in jail." So Faulkner laid the manuscript aside.

Estelle Franklin's divorce was finalized on April 29, 1929, and she and Faulkner were married within a month. But Faulkner expressed his misgivings about his situation in a letter he sent to Hal Smith: "I want $500.00. I am going to be married. Both want to and have to. THIS PART IS CONFIDENTIAL, UTTERLY. For my honor and the sanity—I believe life—of a woman. This is not bunk; neither am I being sucked in. We grew up together and I don't think she could fool me in this way; that is, make me believe that her mental condition, her nerves, are this far gone. . . . It's a situation which I engendered and permitted to ripen which has become unbearable, and I am tired of running from devilment I bring about."

As a divorcee, Estelle could not be married in her family's Episcopal Church, so Faulkner arranged for the pastor of College Hill Presbyterian Church to perform the ceremony. Only the couple, the minister, the minister's wife (as a witness), and Dot were present for the wedding. Using borrowed money and a borrowed car, the couple headed to Pascagoula for their honeymoon, where, according to local reports, both drank profusely. After one drunken argument, Estelle walked into the Gulf of Mexico and tried to drown herself. The couple returned to Oxford, now married as they had thought they would be from childhood, but extremely unhappy. It would seldom be otherwise throughout their long years together.

The Sound and the Fury was published by Jonathan Cape and Harrison Smith on October 7, 1929. It was accompanied by a pamphlet containing a review essay by Evelyn Scott, an established novelist, who compared Faulkner's novel to Greek tragedy. The book, Scott believed, represented "an important contribution to the permanent literature of fiction." Scott was particularly taken by the character of Benjy, the eternal innocent.

Other reviewers were similarly impressed with the novel. One placed Faulkner in the company of Dostoevsky and Joyce; another thought *The Sound and the Fury* equal to a tragedy by Euripides. Favorable reviews also appeared in the prestigious *New York Times* and *Saturday Review of Literature*.

These glowing reviews, however, did not translate into sales. It would take several years for the first printing of less than 2,000 copies of *The Sound and the Fury* to be sold, and the novel would not be reprinted for seventeen years. Thus began a pattern that would be repeated throughout Faulkner's career. His books would be greatly admired by other writers and critics, but would not be bought by the reading public. He was "a writer's writer," someone of whom Hemingway once said, "I would have been happy just to have managed him," but his work was not marketable.

As 1929 drew to a close, Faulkner's personal, emotional, and financial situations were as precarious as they had ever been, but he had now discovered his fictional world of Yoknapatawpha and begun to people it with characters who were as real to him—maybe more real—as the flesh-and-blood people with whom he came in daily contact. As he noted on more than one occasion, in that imaginary world, that "cosmos of [his] own," where he was "sole proprietor," he did not need food, or drink, or sex, or any earthly companion—just pencil and paper and his own creative powers. One of the characters in *Mosquitoes* argues that the principal value of art is found in its power to compensate for and even expel the deficiencies of the actual world: identifying art as "a kind of Battle Creek, Michigan, for the spirit," referring to the famous sanitarium located in that place. Increasingly, Yoknapatawpha would become Faulkner's Battle Creek, and for the rest of his life he would be driven to spend more and more time in its environ. Only there could he ever escape the hurts and anguishes of the world and feel completely fulfilled and happy.

SIX

Genius Unleashed

AFTER THEIR HONEYMOON IN PASCAGOULA AND NEW ORLEANS, Faulkner and Estelle returned to Oxford and moved into a rented apartment on University Avenue, just east of the Ole Miss campus. They furnished it with Estelle's furniture, shipped from Honolulu. Cho-Cho and Malcolm were enrolled in the Oxford school system, and Estelle began her household duties as wife and mother. But the unhappiness that had exploded on the honeymoon quickly returned. Estelle was a loquacious, party-loving person who, in her marriage to Cornell, had had money, a big house, fine clothes, and servants; with Faulkner she was living in genteel poverty with a man who preferred silence and solitude. And both drank: as biographer Stephen Oates puts it, "Faulkner when he wasn't writing, Estelle when he was."

Every day Faulkner would visit his mother, a practice he would regularly follow for the next thirty years whenever he was in Oxford. Initially Estelle accompanied him, but she soon discovered that Maud did not approve of her as a daughter-in-law any more than Lem Oldham approved of Faulkner as his son-in-law. Phil Stone thought all of the Falkner boys were overly dependent on their mother, and Jill Faulkner, years later, following her father's death, echoed that sentiment when she said, "I think that probably Pappy's idea of women—ladies—always revolved a great deal around Granny. She was just a very determined, tiny old lady that Pappy adored. Pappy admired that so much in Granny and he didn't find it in my mother and I don't think he ever found it in anybody. I think that maybe all of these [women] including my mother were, just second place."

Lafayette County Courthouse and confederate statue.

Estelle and Maud Falkner would see a lot of each other over the years, but they never came to like one another, and they seemed always in competition for Faulkner's attention and affection.

To support his new family, Faulkner took a job shoveling coal on the night shift at the university's power plant. He was also writing short stories at a furious pace, but none of them was finding acceptance. This included his best-known story, "A Rose for Emily," which was rejected by *Scribner's*. Some of Faulkner's writing during this period was done during his hours on the night shift. As he later explained, "About 11 o'clock the people would be going to bed, and so it did not take so much steam. Then we could rest, the fireman and I. He would sit in a chair and doze. I had invented a table out of a wheelbarrow in the coal bunker, just beyond a wall from where a dynamo ran. It made a deep, constant humming noise. There was no more work to do until about 4 A.M., when we would have to clean

Rowan Oak, early 1930s.

the fires and get up steam again." This schedule gave him five uninterrupted hours each night in which to write.

It was in this environment that Faulkner wrote *As I Lay Dying*, a novel that many critics feel is the equal of *The Sound and the Fury* in its originality, technical virtuosity, and narrative force. The dates Faulkner entered on the first and last pages of his manuscript reveal that it took him a mere forty-seven days to write the book.

In *The Sound and the Fury* Faulkner had employed four different narrators; in *As I Lay Dying* he utilizes fifteen to tell the story of the Bundren family's difficult, eight-day journey through the Yoknapatawpha countryside to convey the corpse of the wife and mother, Addie, to be buried in her family's cemetery plot in Jefferson. Each narrator has his or her own thoughts about the action, as well as secret thoughts that only the reader learns from the characters' interior monologues. In many respects the Bundrens are a dysfunctional family—Anse, the lazy, shiftless father; Addie, the adulteress;

Cash, the dutiful but repressed son; Darl, the troubled son who is committed to an asylum at the end of the novel; Jewel, the volatile child of Addie and her lover; Dewey Dell, the daughter who is pregnant out of wedlock; and Vardaman, the mentally challenged youngster—but in the course of the novel they endure and prevail over the twin disasters of flood and fire to achieve their goal. And at the end Anse acquires a set of false teeth and a new Mrs. Bundren!

In April 1930, despite his poor financial circumstances, Faulkner purchased the Old Shegog Place, a rundown, neglected antebellum house with four acres of grounds located on Old Taylor Road on the south edge of Oxford. Built in 1849, the house was fronted with four wooden columns and a balcony above the front door. A long, curving drive lined with tall cedars led from the street to the house. Adjacent to the property was a large wooded area known as Bailey's Woods (which Faulkner would later purchase), where Faulkner, Estelle, and many of their friends had often played as children. The purchase price of $6,000 calculated to a mortgage payment of $75 per month.

When the Faulkner family moved into the house, there was no electricity or indoor plumbing. Part of the foundation was rotting away, and the interior rooms needed major repairs and painting. Faulkner immediately set to work doing much of the restoration work himself, using day laborers to assist him. He named the place "Rowan Oak," after the rowan tree that, according to folklore, is reputed to bring good luck.

Soon the Faulkner household would be increased with the addition of two servants, both family retainers of previous generations of the Falkner family: Caroline Barr, who had been the Falkner boys' mammy when they were little, and Ned Barnett, who had worked for the Young Colonel. Mammy Callie helped Estelle with the cooking and housework; Uncle Ned tended the yard, milked the cows, and looked after the horses—and also served as butler on social occasions.

Jill Faulkner later expressed the belief that the ownership of Rowan Oak was crucial to

"Uncle Ned" Barnett.

her father's sense of "being somebody." She continued: "Everybody in Oxford had remembered that Pappy's father ran a livery stable, and he had lived in this house . . . not too far from the livery stable, and this was just a way of thumbing his nose at Oxford . . . [by owning] a nice old house [that] had a certain substance and standing to it." More than one critic would also note parallels between Faulkner and his character Flem Snopes: both rose from poverty to acquire a fine house that served as a symbol of their success and respectability.

Not long after completing *As I Lay Dying* and shipping it off to Hal Smith, to whom the book was dedicated, Faulkner set to work on rewriting the manuscript of *Sanctuary*. As noted previously, Smith had initially thought the story about Mississippi bootleggers and Memphis gangsters that featured the rape of an Ole Miss coed with a corncob too shocking and obscene for the reading public. Now, almost two years later, Smith had changed his mind and decided to publish the book. But when Faulkner received and read the galley proof, he insisted on completely rewriting the book, even if he had to pay for the changes himself. He kept the horror elements, but he toned down the incestuous relationship between Horace and Narcissa and reworked the style and structure. He was pleased with the results—and the reading public was too. Apparently Faulkner had guessed right about what would sell. *Sanctuary*, published on February 9, 1931, became Faulkner's first best seller, going through six printings in five months. Unfortunately, however, Faulkner realized very little money from the sales. The publisher, Jonathan Cape and Harrison Smith, was in financial difficulty and would, in fact, soon close its doors; as a result, Faulkner received very little of the $4,000 in royalties—by some reports, less than $100—that were due him.

Faulkner was beginning, though, to have better luck with his short stories. He had finally succeeded in placing "A Rose for Emily" in *Forum*, "Honor" appeared in *American Mercury*, and the *Saturday Evening Post* took "Thrift" and "Red Leaves," perhaps Faulkner's greatest story about Native Americans. From 1930 to 1932 eighteen of Faulkner's stories appeared in various periodicals, and six of these, plus seven unpublished ones, were collected in *These 13*, published in September 1931.

Faulkner was also attracting critical attention overseas. Chatto and Windus issued an English edition of *Soldiers' Pay* in 1930, and

Arnold Bennett, a well-known British author, wrote a highly favorable review of it. "Faulkner is the coming man," Bennett claimed. "He has inexhaustible invention, powerful imagination, a wondrous gift of characterization, a finished skill in dialogue; and he writes generally like an angel. None of the arrived American stars can surpass him when he is at his best." British editions of *The Sound and the Fury* and *Sanctuary* followed in 1931, and French translations of *Sanctuary* and *As I Lay Dying* appeared, respectively, in 1933 and 1934. (Interestingly, the first French translation of *The Sound and the Fury* did not appear until 1938.)

Faulkner and Estelle's already troubled marriage received a severe blow in January 1931 with the death of their infant daughter Alabama. Born two months premature, Alabama lived only nine days. At that time the Oxford hospital had no incubator, so the parents elected to have the baby cared for by a trained nurse at home. But the child's condition quickly worsened, and by the time Faulkner traveled to Memphis to secure an incubator, it was too late. When Faulkner delivered the news to Estelle that the baby she had never seen had died, he wept bitterly. It was the first time she had ever seen him cry. A few weeks later Faulkner donated an incubator to one of the Oxford clinics, with instructions that it was to be made available without charge to any who could not afford to pay for its use.

The notoriety of *Sanctuary* attracted the attention of Hollywood, where several writers of Faulkner's generation were finding employment, and in May 1932 Faulkner arrived in Tinseltown to begin work as a scriptwriter for Metro-Goldwyn-Mayer. The pay was good—$500 a week for six weeks—but at the end of that time Faulkner had produced nothing that was deemed of great value, and his contract was not renewed. Meanwhile, though, director Howard Hawks had acquired the film rights to Faulkner's World War I short story, "Turn About," and he persuaded Faulkner to help write the screenplay for it. The result was the successful movie *Today We Live*, released in 1933 and starring Gary Cooper, Joan Crawford, Robert Young,

Howard Hawks.

and Franchot Tone. Faulkner and Hawks would collaborate on other film projects in coming years.

Hawks was an avid bird hunter, and Faulkner occasionally joined him on a hunt. On one occasion Hawks also invited Clark Gable, the famous actor, to accompany them. In the course of the conversation Hawks asked Faulkner to identify the greatest living authors. Faulkner replied, "Ernest Hemingway, Willa Cather, Thomas Mann, John Dos Passos, and myself."

Surprised at Faulkner's remark, Gable spoke up: "Oh, Mr. Faulkner, do you write?"

"Yes, Mr. Gable," Faulkner responded. "What do you do?"

Faulkner's work on *Today We Live* was temporarily interrupted when he was called home for the funeral of his father, who died of a heart attack on August 7, 1932. Faulkner and his father had had their differences over the years, but in Murry's final years, Faulkner developed considerable sympathy for him. By now the two men had much in common: they both suffered from a variety of physical and psychological ailments, they were both alcoholics, and they both felt trapped in unhappy marriages. Now that his father was gone, Faulkner would become the head of the family and, as such, would have to assume responsibility for the care of his mother.

In addition to his Hollywood salary, Faulkner also received $6,000 for the sale of the movie rights to *Sanctuary*, which would be filmed as *The Story of Temple Drake*, released in 1933 with Miriam Hopkins playing the title role. Faulkner used some of that money to purchase a Waco biplane from his flight instructor, Captain Vernon Omlie of Memphis. Faulkner had always regretted not having completed his flight training in Toronto during World War I, and he had recently returned to flying. He also paid for flying lessons for his younger brother Dean and granted him free use of the Waco. After Dean finished his schooling and became a professional pilot, he purchased the Waco from Faulkner and used it in air shows.

Light in August, one of Faulkner's greatest works, was published on October 6, 1932. The novel weaves together the stories of three characters: Lena Grove, an unwed pregnant teenager who travels from Alabama to Mississippi looking for the derelict father of her child; Joe Christmas, an orphan who grows into a troubled and violent adult who is unsure of his racial identity but is viewed by the

Faulkner with his Waco, 1930s.

community as a black man; and Gail Hightower, a disgraced minister who is obsessed with his grandfather's death in the Civil War. *Light in August* presents what is perhaps Faulkner's most comprehensive view of life and experience. The tragic story of Christmas, ending with his lynching at the hands of a Jefferson mob, and the religious fanaticism of Simon McEachern and Doc Hines are counterbalanced by the decency of Byron Bunch, the successful quest of Lena, and the redemption of Hightower. No other Faulkner novel better demonstrates the paradoxical nature of life.

Faulkner was now hard at work on another novel that would, even more than *Light in August*, explore the tragic impact of race on southern history. He initially described the book as the story of "a man who outraged the land, and the land then turned and destroyed the man's family." The man was Thomas Sutpen, who rose from poverty to become a plantation owner in antebellum Mississippi. But Sutpen's dream of creating a family dynasty is defeated by events brought on by his rejection of a son who is partly black. For his title Faulkner first considered *Dark House* but eventually chose the lament of King

David in the Old Testament, who, upon hearing that his rebellious son Absalom is dead, cries, "O my son Absalom, O Absalom, my son, my son!" (2 Samuel 19:4) The irony is clear, and telling: David could still love a son who was leading a rebellion against him, but Sutpen could not love a son who is partly black. In such rejection of its black kinsmen, Faulkner saw a principal reason for the tragic history of the South from the days of slavery and the Civil War to the present.

Not content to present Sutpen's story as a standard historical novel, Faulkner achieves an interesting effect in *Absalom, Absalom!* by choosing to have the story told almost a half century later by a number of narrators who know the events largely through rumors and hearsay that have come down from the past—or, as one of the narrators says, through the "rag-tag and bob-ends of old tales and talking." The principal narrator is Quentin Compson, the young suicide of *The Sound and the Fury*, and Quentin's obsession with the Sutpen family narrative not only adds dramatic effect to the present story but also sheds additional light on Quentin's motivation and behavior in the earlier novel. Thus, as he frequently does in the Yoknapatawpha series, Faulkner establishes intertextual links in which one novel or story provides a gloss or commentary on another one. It is one of the distinguishing characteristics of his body of fiction.

Absalom, Absalom! has been called one of the greatest detective stories in American literature. But it is a "whydunit," not a "whodunit." The reader is told early in the story that Henry Sutpen kills Charles Bon, but the actual motive for the killing is withheld until the end of the novel. Meanwhile, various narrators offer conflicting theories about the cause of the murder. Thus what appears to be "true" at one point in the novel becomes false later on, and that pattern is repeated until the final revelation at the end. One early reviewer compared the technique to Faulkner's "story-teller's instinct for circling in, like one of his own bird dogs, on the quarry."

Absalom, Absalom! is an extremely dense, complex novel, one that Faulkner found more challenging to complete than any of his works except the later *A Fable*, which would take him ten years to write. Understandably, he took occasional breaks from the Sutpen story to work on other projects, partly because, as usual, he was strapped for money. He sold a number of short stories to the *Saturday Evening Post* and other magazines, and he chose fourteen of his stories for

Faulkner as pilot, 1930s.

publication in *Dr. Martino and Other Stories*, his second collection of short stories.

His pilot's license now in hand, Faulkner was doing a good bit of solo flying. He also frequently joined his brothers, John and Dean, in participating in air shows. One show in Ripley was advertised in circulars as "William Faulkner's (Famous Author) Air Circus." Faulkner also, with Dean and Omlie as copilots, flew the Waco to New York to meet with his publishers.

In February 1934 Faulkner attended the air races that were part of the ceremony dedicating the Shushan Airport in New Orleans. There were several crashes during the races, one of which claimed the life of a pilot. Faulkner was fascinated with the dangerous and nomadic lifestyle of the barnstormers, years later recollecting "those frantic little aeroplanes which dashed around the country and people [who] wanted just enough money to live, to get to the next place to race again."

After viewing the air show in New Orleans Faulkner set aside the partial manuscript of *Absalom, Absalom!* to write a novel about the barnstorming pilots. As Faulkner later explained, "I'd got in trouble with *Absalom, Absalom!* and I had to get away from it for a while." Unlike the writing of *Absalom, Absalom!*, that of *Pylon* came easily and quickly, and the novel was published on March 25, 1935. The story ends with the death of one of the main characters, Roger Shumann, in a plane crash much like the one in New Orleans.

The fictional fate of Roger Shumann proved tragically prophetic a few months later. On November 10, 1935, during an air show in Pontotoc, thirty miles east of Oxford, Dean Falkner and three others died in the crash of the Waco that Faulkner had provided him. Faulkner drove to Pontotoc to accompany his brother's corpse back to Oxford. He would be haunted the rest of his life by what he found and did there. "Dean was so badly disfigured," Faulkner said later, "that I spent the whole night with the mortician at the side of a bathtub trying to put his face back in some shape." For months afterward Faulkner experienced horrible nightmares, and he would never forgive himself for encouraging Dean to become a pilot and allowing him to purchase the Waco.

Dean left behind a young widow, Louise, who was four months pregnant. When the baby girl was born, she was named Dean, after her dad. Faulkner became her surrogate father, providing for her in childhood, welcoming her to live from time to time at Rowan Oak, paying for her education, and giving her away in marriage. To his niece, Faulkner would always be simply "Pappy," just as he was to Jill, Malcolm, and Cho-Cho.

Added to Faulkner's grief over the death of his brother was the escalating conflict within his marriage. Estelle was still finding it difficult to adjust to Faulkner's habits as a writer who lived much of the time in his own private thoughts. Sometimes, especially if Faulkner were involved in a writing project, meals would be spent in utter silence. Faulkner had a room, which he called his "office," added to Rowan Oak, and he often secluded himself there to write. Estelle busied herself with domestic chores, but she wanted to dine out, see friends, party, dance, and travel. She played the piano and developed an interest in painting, but these activities failed to relieve her terrible boredom. Like Faulkner, though for quite different reasons, she drank, excessively.

The birth of their sole surviving child, Jill, in 1933, brought the couple closer for a while, but soon the hurt, anger, and recriminations resumed. Estelle spent money they didn't have, running up huge debts for expensive clothes and furniture. As her spendthrift ways continued, Faulkner placed an announcement in the Oxford and Memphis papers that he would not be responsible for any more of her debts.

In December 1935 Faulkner heeded the call of Howard Hawks and returned to Hollywood to assist screenwriter Joel Sayre in writing the script for *The Road to Glory*, a World War I movie. Released in 1936, the film is today considered a classic war movie, partly because of the actual battle footage that Hawks spliced into the scenes. Faulkner and Sayre received joint screen credit for the script.

Faulkner and Jill, 1934.

While working on *The Road to Glory*, Faulkner met Meta Carpenter, who worked as a secretary and script girl in Hawks's office. Faulkner was immediately captivated by her. Twenty-eight years old, delicate, cultured, and beautiful, Meta was a transplanted Mississippian, having grown up in Tunica, in the Delta. An unfortunate early marriage had ended in divorce, and now Meta was making her way as an independent, professional woman in the world of Hollywood. She would eventually work in the movie industry for fifty years, in the course of her career assisting directors like Hawks and Mike Nichols and stars such as Richard Burton and Elizabeth Taylor in their work. She also worked on the filming of Faulkner's novel *The Reivers* in 1969.

Faulkner, mid-1930s.

Faulkner and Meta quickly became lovers. Unhappy at home, but lonely and insecure in Hollywood, Faulkner was open to an extramarital affair. In the book that she later wrote about the relationship, Meta explained, "I could make him forget for hours on end that he was so far from home.

Meta Carpenter.

Faulkner and Meta Carpenter, Los Angeles, 1935.

Together we recreated our own South. It helped make his life away from Oxford endurable."

What started as a casual affair soon developed into a serious relationship that would continue, intermittently, for fifteen years. Faulkner confessed his love for Meta and promised that he would marry her after he secured a divorce from Estelle. He told Ben Wasson, "That's the girl I'm in love with. Can't get her out of my mind or system. And don't want to. . . . I want to marry Meta." The only obstacle, Faulkner told Meta, was the issue of the custody of Jill. For her part, Meta gave herself fully to Faulkner and agreed to wait for him.

Faulkner continued working on *Absalom, Absalom!* while in Hollywood, typically writing in the early morning hours before reporting to the studio for his screenwriting duties. When the novel was finished, he handed the manuscript to a fellow screenwriter, David Hempstead, with the remark, "I think it's the best novel yet written by an American." He made final corrections to the manuscript back home in Oxford, and the book was published on October 26, 1936.

Absalom, Absalom! was the first of Faulkner's major works to be published by Random House, which had invited Hal Smith and Robert Haas, Faulkner's current publishers, to join the larger firm.

Faulkner at writing desk, Rowan Oak, 1936.

Bennett Cerf, the head of Random House, had courted Faulkner for several years, telling him at one point that he could write his own ticket if he would contract with Random House. "I think we'd rather have you on our list than any other fiction writer living in America," Cerf wrote to Faulkner. Later, Cerf explained, "We didn't think he'd *ever* be a commercial success, but he would be the greatest possible adornment to the Random House list." Eventually, of course, both Random House and Faulkner were amply rewarded for their partnership.

One of the unexpected benefits of Faulkner's joining Random House was his close friendship with Saxe Commins, the editor initially assigned to oversee Faulkner's work. As a minor partner at Random House, Commins sometimes felt neglected and under-appreciated—an ironical situation, given that the two major authors Commins worked with were Eugene O'Neill and Faulkner, both of whom would become Nobel Prize winners. Commins and Faulkner quickly bonded, and in the years afterward Commins became Faulkner's confidant, advisor, and benefactor. On one occasion Commins, who suffered from a serious heart condition, risked his own health to nurse Faulkner through a drunken stupor in a New York hotel. No individual was closer to Faulkner, or more crucial to his career, in his later years than Commins.

Welcoming guests to Rowan Oak, 1938.

Despite the money he had made in Hollywood, Faulkner was still heavily in debt. Moreover, given the difficulty of the text, *Absalom, Absalom!* was not likely to sell in substantial numbers. Perhaps, Faulkner reasoned, he could produce a book that would have more popular appeal. Utilizing a tactic he would later repeat in producing *The Hamlet* and *Go Down, Moses*, he recycled a number of magazine stories, reworking them and shaping them into a novel. In this case it was the six stories about the Civil War and Reconstruction exploits of John Sartoris and Granny Millard, and about the developing relationship of Bayard Sartoris with his African American playmate, Ringo. To these Faulkner added a concluding chapter, "An Odor of Verbena," one of Faulkner's finest narratives. The result was *The Unvanquished*, published on February 15, 1938. In later years this was the book Faulkner always recommended as the starting point for readers of his fiction.

SEVEN

Farmer

———————— ◦◦ ————————

IN 1938 FAULKNER SOLD THE FILM RIGHTS TO *THE UNVANQUISHED*
to Metro-Goldwyn-Mayer for $25,000 and used the money he netted
from the sale to purchase a farm. Located seventeen miles northeast
of Oxford, it comprised 320 acres, with pine thickets covering the
hillsides and several acres of arable bottomland. He named the place
Greenfield Farm.

The farm had originally belonged to Joe Parks, who some years
earlier had moved into Oxford, purchased Murry Falkner's house,
and eventually seized control of Faulkner's grandfather's bank. Now
Faulkner had a bit of revenge. He would have even more in making
Joe Parks one of the prototypes of Flem Snopes, one of Faulkner's
most famous villains.

Faulkner's purchase of Greenfield Farm allowed him to continue a
family tradition. His father had owned a farm, as had his grandfather
and great-grandfather. But Faulkner's desire to own a farm was in-
tensely personal: he had always felt a spiritual kinship with the land,
and now he had a place to ride and hunt and immerse himself in the
colors and textures of the changing seasons. John Faulkner thought
there was an additional motive for his brother's action. "Bill found
more than just a farm out there," John wrote. "He found the kind of
people he wrote about, hill people." Whatever the reason, Faulkner
derived great satisfaction from owning Greenfield Farm. "I'm not
a literary man," he liked to say from this point forward. "I'm just a
farmer who likes to tell stories."

William Faulkner, 1930s.

Faulkner hired his brother John to manage the farm. John recommended raising cattle, but Faulkner preferred mules. In his first Yoknapatawpha novel he had written: "Some Cincinnatus of the cotton fields should contemplate the lowly destiny, some Homer should sing the saga, of the mule and of his place in the South. He it was, more than any one creature or thing, who, steadfast to the land when all else faltered before the hopeless juggernaut of circumstance, impervious to conditions that broke men's hearts because of his venomous and patient preoccupation with the immediate present, won the prone South from beneath the iron heel of Reconstruction and taught it pride again through humility and courage through adversity overcome. . . ." Faulkner's fondness for mules notwithstanding, the commitment to raising and selling them proved to be a bad business decision, since tractors were already beginning to displace mules on southern farms. But Faulkner was adamant. As John recalled, "He said he had no feeling for cows. He wanted brood mares and a tack room with riding equipment in it. So we raised mules."

John enlisted a number of African American families as tenants, and Faulkner contributed Uncle Ned Barnett to the work force. By this time Uncle Ned, like Mammy Callie, had become almost a member of the Faulkner family. Indeed, when Faulkner revised his last will and testament in 1940, he included a provision that would grant to Uncle Ned the privilege of living on at Greenfield Farm, rent free, until his death. The provision was much like the one old Carothers McCaslin makes for Lucas Beauchamp in a later Faulkner novel, *Go Down, Moses.* However, Uncle Ned didn't live out his years at Greenfield Farm; when in his old age he expressed a desire to move "back home" to Ripley, Faulkner arranged for him to so, continuing to provide for the old servant until his death.

The Faulkners opened a commissary at Greenfield Farm to provide staple goods for the tenants. Once, in visiting the farm, Faulkner noticed that John had raised the prices on the goods sold there, since,

Faulkner with his brother John.

as John explained, the supplier had increased his prices. Faulkner told John to mark the prices back down, since "it was not the Negroes' fault that prices went up and he wasn't going to penalize them for it."

Faulkner also had a small private lodge built on the property that he used for overnight visits and occasionally for reading and writing. Nestled at the top of a long slope, the lodge allowed Faulkner to sit on the screened-in porch and have a good view of the tenants moving about the farm.

Even as Faulkner settled into farm ownership, he made rapid advances on his current work in progress, *If I Forget Thee, Jerusalem*. All of the editors at Random House were lobbying against that title, a quotation from the 137th Psalm, and Faulkner finally acceded to their wishes, changing the title to *The Wild Palms*. The book exhibited Faulkner's constant willingness to experiment with narrative form, presenting what appear to be two separate stories arranged as successively alternating chapters. On close analysis, however, the stories evidence a close interrelationship, as identical themes of love, flight, and imprisonment are employed in both the Charlotte

Rittenmeyer–Harry Wilbourne story and the episode of the tall convict. Faulkner called the method of presentation "contrapuntal," employing the concept of counterpoint borrowed from musical composition.

In January 1939 Faulkner was elected to the National Institute of Arts and Letters, and the January 23 issue of *Time* magazine featured a photograph of him on the cover and a story about his life and work. Although Faulkner typically avoided publicity, in this instance he fully cooperated with the author of the piece, Robert Cantwell, perhaps because Cantwell was a fellow novelist. Faulkner met Cantwell in Memphis and drove him to Oxford, talked freely with him about the Old Colonel and about himself, and introduced Cantwell to Mammy Callie. He even allowed Cantwell to photograph him with Jill on her bicycle. It is one of only a few Faulkner photographs in which he is smiling.

About this same time Faulkner was called upon to help an old friend. Phil Stone's father had died, passing on to his son considerable debt. Needing several thousand dollars to avoid foreclosure on one note, Stone appealed to Faulkner for assistance. Faulkner was in poor financial shape himself, but he could not refuse to help the man who had meant so much to him both personally and professionally. Securing a royalty advance from Random House and also cashing in a life insurance policy, he gave the money to Stone, $6,000 in all. Stone never repaid the money, and Faulkner never asked him to do so.

Faulkner occasionally visited Greenfield Farm to go bird hunting with John and John's sons, Jimmy and Chooky. He also started a tradition of having a Fourth of July barbecue at the farm for all the tenants and invited guests. Workers dug a hole in the ground, filled it with hickory wood, and started the fire. Faulkner assisted with the cooking and basting, using his own special barbecue sauce on the meat. The tenants sang as guests sat under the trees, eating and drinking.

Faulkner was now at work on a novel he initially called *The Peasants*, a title borrowed from one of his favorite authors, Honoré de Balzac, the French writer whose multivolume *La Comédie humaine* (*The Human Comedy*) is thought by many to be a model for Faulkner's Yoknapatawpha series. Published in 1940 as *The Hamlet*, it would become the first of three volumes devoted to the Snopes clan. Fleshing out the story he had years earlier conceived as *Father Abraham*, and incorporating a number of short stories he had recently written, Faulkner traced the steady rise of Flem Snopes, the shrewd and conniving son of a barn-burning sharecropper. Flem clerks in Will Varner's country store, cuts a business deal with Varner by marrying his pregnant daughter Eula, conspires with a Texan to sell untamable horses to his neighbors, and fleeces other characters by means of the old "salted mine" trick. By the end of the novel Flem has displaced Varner as the most powerful individual in Frenchman's Bend and is preparing to move on to bigger challenges in Jefferson. *The Hamlet* is one of Faulkner's funniest novels, and perhaps his most underrated one.

As Faulkner worked on the Snopes story, he was also "boiling the pot," as he called it, creating short stories and sending them off to magazines. "Barn Burning," one of his finest stories, was accepted by *Harper's* and "Hand upon the Waters" by the *Saturday Evening*

Mammy Callie (Caroline Barr).

Post. Faulkner needed this money badly, as his aid to Phil Stone had placed him once again in difficult financial straits.

In January 1940 Mammy Callie, Faulkner's "other mother," died. Her funeral was held in the parlor at Rowan Oak, and Faulkner delivered the eulogy. "From her," Faulkner said, "I learned to tell the truth, to refrain from waste, to be considerate of the weak and respectful to age." She demonstrated "fidelity to a family which was not hers, devotion and love for people she had not borne." Faulkner concluded, "If there is a heaven, she has gone there." Mammy Callie was buried in St. Peter's cemetery, not far from the Falkner family plot. Her memorial stone reads: "MAMMY / Her white children / bless her."

As he waited for *The Hamlet* to make its way through the publication process, Faulkner resumed "boiling the pot," turning out stories for the magazines. One group of these may have been partly influenced by his stewardship of Greenfield Farm and his close interaction with its African American tenants. These were stories about four generations of the McCaslin family and the blacks, some of whom were relatives through miscegenation, who lived on the McCaslin plantation. Also included were stories, principally "The Bear" and "Delta Autumn," that exhibit Faulkner's great love of the land and his regret over how it was being exploited and destroyed by modernization.

As he had done with the Snopes stories in writing *The Hamlet*, Faulkner recognized in the McCaslin stories the germ of a novel. It would be called *Go Down, Moses*, after the old Negro spiritual, and it would trace the descendants of Lucius Quintus Carothers McCaslin ("Old McCaslin"), white and black, from antebellum days into the 1940s. Though the novel would reflect a degree of skepticism about whites and blacks ever coming to a harmonious understanding and acceptance (as in the conflict between Lucas Beauchamp and Zack Edmonds in "The Fire and the Hearth," the deputy sheriff's misguided response to Rider's behavior in "Pantaloon in Black," and Gavin Stevens's confused reaction at the funeral service of Samuel Beauchamp in "Go Down, Moses"), the book represents Faulkner's most sympathetic treatment of the African Americans' rise from slavery and their quest for equality and dignity. Faulkner dedicated the book to Mammy Caroline Barr, "who was born in slavery and who gave to my family a fidelity without stint or calculation of recompense and to my childhood an immeasurable devotion and love."

By now the United States was well into World War II, and Faulkner watched his stepson, Malcolm, and his favorite nephew, Jimmy, head off to basic training. Malcolm would serve as a combat medic in Europe, and Jimmy would become a marine fighter pilot. Faulkner himself tried to enlist but was judged too old for active service. A number of the stories he wrote at this time drew upon the wartime setting. In "The Tall Men" the sons of a hill farmer fail to register for the draft but readily volunteer to serve their country. In "Two Soldiers" a ten-year-old boy follows his older brother to the enlistment center and seeks to accompany his brother overseas. In "Shall Not Perish" a mother who has lost a son in the war travels into Jefferson to commiserate with another parent whose son has been killed.

As productive as he was in the late thirties and early forties, Faulkner was still not earning a living from his writing—or from the farm. The royalties from *The Wild Palms* and *The Hamlet* barely covered the cash advances Faulkner had already received; the magazine sales were too infrequent and, except for those to *The Saturday Evening Post*, not very profitable; and a military appointment had been denied. As his debts mounted and his income declined, Faulkner sought the one financial option that seemed open to him: he wrote to his agent Harold Ober and asked him to try to find work for him again in Hollywood.

EIGHT

Golden Land

IN MAY 1942, AT AGE FORTY-FOUR, WILLIAM FAULKNER SHOULD have been the happiest author in America. He had just published *Go Down, Moses*, concluding a decade-plus run of creativity that has seldom been matched in literary history. Between 1929 and 1942, he had published eleven novels, two collections of short stories, more than fifty individual short stories in such prestigious periodicals as *Saturday Evening Post*, *Harper's*, *Scribner's Magazine*, and *American Mercury*, and a second volume of poetry. Three of the novels—*The Sound and the Fury*, *As I Lay Dying*, and *Light in August*—now appear on the *New York Times* list of the one hundred greatest novels; and many scholars believe that *Absalom, Absalom!* also belongs on the list. To find anything resembling the concentrated and sustained level of creative genius represented by this period of Faulkner's life, one would have to look at the careers of such writers as, say, Henry James, or Charles Dickens, or perhaps even Shakespeare. Indeed, Faulkner has sometimes been called "the American Shakespeare."

Yet he was not happy; in fact, he was miserable—and flat broke. His books were not selling, he was heavily in debt to local merchants and in arrears on his income tax payments, he felt trapped in an unhappy marriage, and he was drinking heavily. He tried, unsuccessfully, to enlist in the military, as much to have a regular paycheck as to perform his patriotic duty during wartime. In a letter to his publisher he wrote: "I have 60c in my pocket, and that is literally all. I finished a story and sent it in yesterday, but with no real hope it will sell. My local creditors bother me, but so far none has taken an action because I

EMPLOYEE'S STARTING RECORD — WARNER BROS. PICTURES, INC		
MAN NO. _____	SOCIAL SECURITY NO. _548-05-8158_	
DATE _7-27-42_	NAME _FAULKNER, WILLIAM_	
HOUR STARTED_____	ADDRESS_____	
RATE _300._	CITY_____	
_____	PHONE_____	
DEPARTMENT_____	OCCUPATION _Writer_	
DATE OF BIRTH_____	PLACE OF BIRTH_____	
NATIONALITY_____	MARRIED____ SINGLE____	
LEGAL RES. (STATE)_____	CITIZEN OF U.S.____	
IF NOT CITIZEN (DATE OF ENTRY)_____	QUOTA NO.____	
UNION_____	EVER EMPLOYED HERE BEFORE____	
13 weeks - 3 idle. (Make MPRF deductions)		
APPROVED_ R. ___RINGER_	EMPLOYEE'S SIGNATURE	
ML-149		

Faulkner's starting record for Warner Bros. Studios, 1942.

began last year to give them notes for debts. But the notes will come due soon and should I be sued, my whole house here will collapse: farm, property, everything." He had been depressed and discouraged before in his life, but never this badly.

In desperation, both financially and emotionally, he sought to return to Hollywood, on whatever terms could be arranged. William Herndon, a young and inexperienced agent, secured a scriptwriting job for him at Warner Bros. Studio, although, because of Faulkner's reputation as a heavy drinker, the pay would be only $300 per week (less than half of his previous salary in Hollywood) and although, as Faulkner would later learn to his chagrin, Herndon had had to agree to a series of options that would keep Faulkner contractually tied to Warner Bros. for seven years. Still, it was work, and he had no better options.

On a happier note, returning to Hollywood afforded him the opportunity to resume his relationship with Meta Carpenter. Meta had given up on waiting for Faulkner and had married Wolfgang Rebner, a concert pianist, but the marriage had not lasted, because, some believed, she was still in love with Faulkner. Meta had heard that Faulkner was coming back to Hollywood, but she didn't yet know the date. Then, one evening, driving up to her apartment, she found Faulkner sitting on her front steps. They went to their favorite restaurant, Musso and Frank's, for dinner. Meta had long since given up her dream that Faulkner would one day marry her, but she was glad to have him back in her life. And Faulkner needed Meta in his, now more than ever.

Faulkner's first assignment for Warner Bros. was to author an original screenplay on the career of General Charles De Gaulle, the leader of the Free French forces and an American ally against Germany in World War II. Given the antiwar movies of the Vietnam and post-Vietnam eras, it is hard to imagine that during World War II Hollywood became a virtual propaganda agency for the U.S. government. Jack Warner, a close friend of President Roosevelt, was a willing partner in this arrangement; and William Faulkner, who had been recently judged too old for wartime service, found an expression of his patriotism by writing scripts that supported the war effort.

Over a four-month period, incorporating information and advice from Free French consultants representing General De Gaulle, Faulkner produced a story outline, initial and expanded story treatments, and two different versions of a completed screenplay. Despite all of Faulkner's hard work and high hopes, however, the De Gaulle project was cancelled and never filmed.

There were several reasons that *The De Gaulle Story* never made it to the screen, none of which seems to have had much to do with the quality of Faulkner's script. Most importantly, there was the ongoing conflict between Faulkner and the Free French consultants regarding the focus of the script. The Gaullists wanted the film to be primarily a biography of Charles De Gaulle, whereas Faulkner wanted to focus on ordinary French citizens (in the script, two brothers) caught up in the conflict between the Free French and the Vichy French. Eventually, becoming more and more exasperated by the consultants' unwillingness to compromise, Faulkner sent a memo to the film's producer, Robert Buckner, recommending: "Let's dispense with General De Gaulle as a living character in the story. . . . If we use him as a living character, we must accept the supervision of his representatives, and at least satisfy them, even if we can't please them. Being Free Frenchmen and working for a tough cause, they are naturally more interested in the progress of the cause than in a mere American made and financed . . . moving picture. They want to see a piece of Free French propaganda, not a moving picture in which

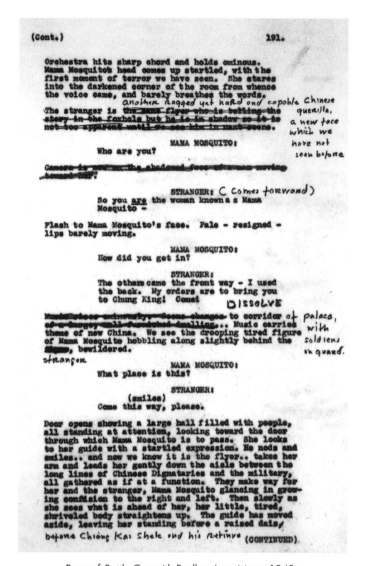

(Cont.)   191.

Orchestra hits sharp chord and holds ominous.
Mama Mosquitos head comes up startled, with the
first moment of terror we have seen. She stares
into the darkened corner of the room from whence
the voice came, and barely breathes the words.
another ragged yet hard and capable Chinese
The stranger is ~~the man flyer who is telling the~~ *querilla,*
~~story in the foxhole but he is in shadow so it is~~ *a new face*
~~not too apparent until we see him in next scene.~~ *which we*
have not
seen before

                              MAMA MOSQUITO:
            Who are you?

~~Camera is now on the abandoned face as it is moving~~
~~toward us.~~

                              STRANGER: (*Comes forward*)
            So you **are** the woman known a s Mama
            Mosquito -

Flash to Mama Mosquito's face. Pale - resigned -
lips barely moving.

                              MAMA MOSQUITO:
            How did you get in?

                              STRANGER:
            The others came the front way - I used
            the back. My orders are to bring you
            to Chung King! Come!   DISSOLVE

~~Music Picture minously. Scene changes~~ to corridor of *palace,*
~~of a large well-furnished dwelling...~~ Music carries *with*
theme of new China. We see the drooping tired figure *soldiers*
of Mama Mosquito hobbling along slightly behind the *on guard.*
~~man,~~ bewildered.
stranger
                              MAMA MOSQUITO:
            What place is this?

                              STRANGER:
                  (smiles)
            Come this way, please.

Door opens showing a large hall filled with people,
all standing at attention, looking toward the door
through which Mama Mosquito is to pass. She looks
to her guide with a startled expression. He nods and
smiles.. and now we know it is the flyer.. takes her
arm and leads her gently down the aisle between the
long lines of Chinese Dignataries and the military,
all gathered as if at a function. They make way for
her and the stranger, Mama Mosquito glancing in growing confusion to the right and left. Then slowly as
she sees what is ahead of her, her little, tired,
shriveled body straightens up. The guide has moved
aside, leaving her standing before a raised dais,
before Chiang Kai Shek and his retinue (CONTINUED).

Page of *Battle Cry*, with Faulkner's revisions, 1943.

those who see it will recognize their own human passions and griefs and desires."

In addition to the recalcitrance of the Gaullists, shifting war-time politics also contributed to the cancellation of the project. Increasingly, De Gaulle had become troublesome to the Allied cause, and President Roosevelt and Prime Minister Churchill had begun to exclude the Frenchman from their military strategies. As a result, by mid-November 1942, the date of Faulkner's last work on the project, a movie about the leader of the French Underground had ceased being a major priority, first for the U.S. government and consequently for Warner Bros., the movie studio most closely aligned with the national defense effort.

While Faulkner was greatly disappointed over the termination of the De Gaulle project, his hopes were renewed a short time later with the invitation to work on Howard Hawks's proposed epic film celebrating the combined war efforts of the Allied forces. Faulkner expressed his enthusiasm for this assignment in a letter home to his daughter Jill: "I am writing a big picture now, for Mr Howard Hawks, an old friend, a director. It is to be a big one. It will last about 3 hours, and the studio has allowed Mr Hawks 3 and 1/2 million dollars to make it, with 3 or 4 directors and about all the big stars. It will probably be named 'Battle Cry.'"

Understandably, Faulkner thought that his work on *Battle Cry* would allow him to escape his precarious financial situation. His confidence is reflected in one letter he wrote Estelle: "[Hawks] is going to establish his own unit, as an independent: himself, his writer, etc., to write pictures, then sell them to any studio who makes highest bid. I am to be his writer. He says he and I together as a team will always be worth two million dollars at least. That means, we can count on getting at least two million from any studio with which to make any picture we cook up, we to make the picture with the two million dollars, and divide the profits from it. When I come home, I intend to have Hawks completely satisfied with this job, as well as the studio. If I can do that, I won't have to worry again about going broke temporarily." Faulkner went on to describe *Battle Cry* as "something I believe in" and to note that "now that [he had] written a good picture," he should be able to negate the onerous contract to which Herndon had committed him.

Once again, however, Faulkner's hopes were dashed. When the budget office concluded that it would cost at least $4,000,000 to produce the epic film, the studio closed the project down. Thus for the second time in twelve months, a project for which Faulkner held high hopes—both financially and artistically—was terminated, and all the writing he had done for both projects was buried in the studio's vaults.

With the demise of *Battle Cry*, the little enthusiasm Faulkner had managed to summon for this round of Hollywood work disappeared, and he searched for ways to void his contract. He tried unsuccessfully to negotiate a settlement with the agent Herndon, and he begged Jack Warner to release him from his contract with Warner Bros. But Warner, who was known to refer to writers as "schmucks with typewriters," refused Faulkner's request.

Meanwhile, Faulkner continued his affair with Meta. They dined out, strolled together along Hollywood Boulevard, went to the beach, and occasionally attended dinner parties with close friends. Meta offered to let Faulkner move into her apartment, but he declined. He told her it was because of his "Southern rectitude," but it may have been because he feared domesticity as a result of his life back in Oxford.

Not all of Faulkner's free time, however, was spent in the company of Meta, and she began to notice a distancing in their relationship. He went hunting and fishing with Howard Hawks and Clark Gable. He spent time with producer Robert Buckner and his family. He liked to visit actress Ruth Ford and her daughter, Shelley. A few years earlier Ruth had been a student at Ole Miss and had dated Dean Falkner for a while.

Faulkner's disappointment over the cancellations of *The De Gaulle Story* and *Battle Cry* was immense, but his Hollywood luck was about to change for the better; and, as was the case a decade earlier, Howard Hawks was the catalyst. In early 1944 Hawks persuaded Warner Bros. to produce a film based on Ernest Hemingway's novel *To Have and Have Not*. Hawks first enlisted a well-known screenwriter, Jules Furthman, to write the screen adaptation, but when Furthman left the project to work on another film, Hawks secured Faulkner to revise Furthman's script.

To Have and Have Not, in both Hemingway's novel and Furthman's adaptation, recounts the story of Harry Morgan, a down-and-nearly-out fishing boat captain who survives the Great Depression by using his charter boat to smuggle liquor,

Faulkner in Hollywood, 1940s.

illegal immigrants, and revolutionaries between Cuba and Key West. Faulkner, however, apprised of the U.S. government's sensitivity to political developments in Cuba and coming fresh from the French material he had used in *The De Gaulle Story* and *Battle Cry*, persuaded Hawks to recast Hemingway's story as a World War II drama depicting the conflict of the Free French and Vichy French. To support this reinterpretation, Hawks shifted the setting from Cuba to the island of Martinique, a French province under the control of the Vichy government. This reshaping of Hemingway's novel produced two significant effects, one dramatic and one commercial. In Faulkner's handling of the story Morgan, by risking his life in support of the Free French cause, is presented with a means of moral redemption lacking in the Hemingway characterization. In addition, the shift of focus enabled Humphrey Bogart, as Morgan, to reprise the Free French role that had been such a great success in the recent Warner Bros. film *Casablanca* (1942).

Faulkner shared with Furthman the screen credit for the script of *To Have and Have Not*, and his success on that project led to his assignment to work on the film adaptation of Raymond Chandler's mystery thriller, *The Big Sleep*, which starred Bogart and Lauren Bacall, as had *To Have and Have Not*. Leigh Brackett, a young, relatively inexperienced screenwriter, was assigned to work with Faulkner, and Hawks directed them to deliver a script with lots of action and witty dialogue. The two writers succeeded admirably on both counts, but their ending was both overlong and unacceptable to the censors, who took issue with the hero of the story deliberately allowing another character—even if she is a murderess, a nymphomaniac, and a drug addict—to walk into a trap and be shot to death. So Hawks called in Furthman to rewrite the ending, the result being that all three writers received a film credit for the screenplay. *The Big Sleep* remains Faulkner's most successful and best known film; in 1997 the United States National Film Preservation Board deemed the movie "culturally, historically, or aesthetically significant" and listed it for inclusion in the National Film Registry at the Library of Congress.

Two events that occurred toward the end of Faulkner's Warner Bros. tenure would have long-lasting effects upon his literary career. The first was an invitation from producer William Bacher and director Henry Hathaway to collaborate on a possible movie based on the stories that had circulated about the Unknown Soldier of World War I. While the idea for such a movie was subsequently abandoned, Faulkner's discussions with Bacher and Hathaway planted the seeds for his subsequent writing of *A Fable*, in which the French Unknown Soldier is conjectured to be Jesus Christ, who has returned to earth only to be crucified a second time.

The second event was the receipt of a letter from Malcolm Cowley, a well-known poet and critic, who expressed a desire to edit a representative collection of Faulkner's works for Viking Press's Portable Authors series. Cowley had previously edited *The Portable Hemingway*, and now he wanted to do the same for Faulkner. *The Portable Faulkner*, which would appear a year later, has been credited for resurrecting Faulkner's career by making his works readily available to the reading public.

Faulkner's last work for Warner Bros. before he walked out on his contract, a screen adaptation of Stephen Longstreet's novel *Stallion Road*, is instructive in both his acquired competence as a scenarist, as well as some of the obstacles to his ultimate success in that medium. Faulkner's compatibility with the themes of Longstreet's novel—love of horses, preference for a rural and small-town way of life, a skeptical attitude toward modern "progress," an admiration of common, ordinary citizens, a celebration of individual rather than collective values, a contempt for rampant materialism and greed—undoubtedly contributed to Faulkner's success in authoring the screenplay. But in converting the novel to a script, Faulkner also faced a number of challenging issues.

First and foremost, of course, was the necessity to compress the 300-page novel into a 75-minute movie script. Faulkner accomplished this task primarily by eliminating characters, deleting or combining scenes, and, crucially, ignoring the lengthy editorial passages in Longstreet's pages. The result was a streamlined plot centered on one main character, Larry Hanrahan, and the two women in love with him (as opposed to the novel's presentation of two main characters with multiple sex/love interests), as well as an altered communication of theme by indirection and implication instead of direct preachments.

While Faulkner's compression of Longstreet's novel into a unified, artistic script was successful, his handling of the realistic details of

Warner Bros. off payroll notice for Faulkner.

his plot failed to get past Hays Code censors. In his evaluation of Faulkner's initial version of the screenplay Joseph I. Breen, the director of the Production Code Administration of the Motion Picture Producers and Distributors of America, informed Warner Bros. that several changes would be required. For one thing, all of the scenes involving animals would have to conform to the standards of the American Humane Society. A more serious concern related to the adulterous affair between Hanrahan and Daisy Otis. Breen advised, "Kindly keep down to a minimum all scenes of kissing or embracing between Mrs. Otis and Larry."

Despite Breen's expressions of concern, Faulkner did not abridge the sexual elements of the story. In his final version of the script Daisy is still the aggressive, uninhibited nymphomaniac, and she and Larry continue to flaunt their adulterous relationship in public. In addition, Daisy and Fleece, the rival for Hanrahan's affection, engage in a relentless and often prurient repartee of sexual innuendoes and double entendres. It was primarily these aspects of the plot that Stephen Longstreet had in mind when he said that Faulkner's script was "a little strong for then." Predictably, the unconventional sexual details are missing from the next version of the screenplay, written by Emmet Lavery, and from the film version scripted by Longstreet.

Jill on Lady Go-lightly, Glendale, California, 1944.

While Faulkner's version of *Stallion Road* represents one of his most artful movie scripts, it also provides evidence that, in the Hollywood of 1945, Faulkner was considerably ahead of his time.

Without even cleaning out his desk, Faulkner walked out on his Warner Bros. contract on December 13, 1945, and went home to Oxford. In addition to being fed up with Jack Warner and William Herndon, he was worried about not ever being able to complete his "big book," the Christ fable, if he stayed in Hollywood. "I'll never get it written if I stay in this town," he told Meta. "Sometimes I think if I do one more treatment or screenplay, I'll lose whatever power I have as a writer."

Faulkner had one last chore to perform before he left Hollywood. Estelle and Jill had joined him for his last summer there, and he and Jill frequently went riding at one of the local stables. Jill had fallen in love with one of the horses, named Lady Go-lightly. Now Faulkner purchased the horse for Jill, bought a trailer, and hired a driver to deliver the animal and the writer to Rowan Oak. Arriving in Oxford, Faulkner watched with delight as Jill raced to embrace Lady Go-lightly. "It's my horse!" she exclaimed. "It's my horse!"

NINE

Return to Yoknapatawpha

BACK HOME, FAULKNER WROTE WARNER REQUESTING AGAIN that the remaining years of his contract be cancelled. "I feel that I have made a bust at moving picture writing and therefore have mis-spent and will continue to mis-spend time which at my age I cannot afford." The studio wrote back to say no, and to remind him that Warner Bros. retained control of anything he wrote during the term of his contract. He would be granted a six-months' leave, but after that time he would be expected to return to the studio.

Despite his business problems, he was glad to be home again. He was with Jill and family again, and he went horseback riding and deer hunting with old friends. He oversaw the harvest season at Greenfield Farm. Christmas that year at Rowan Oak brought special joy. Nephew Jimmy Faulkner and stepson Malcolm Franklin were home from the war. Dressed formally as they always did for Christmas, Faulkner and Estelle passed out gifts to the family on Christmas morning and hosted visits from friends that afternoon. All too soon the problems would return—his conflict with Warner Bros., his struggle with the fable, the unhappy marriage, his heavy drinking—but on this Christmas Faulkner, surrounded by family and friends, was more contented than he had been in a long time.

Faulkner, 1940s.

Lafayette County Courthouse, 1940s.

Jill and Lady Go-lightly, c. 1945.

The new year brought Faulkner a bit of welcome news. His agent Harold Ober and Random House persuaded Warner Bros. to allow Faulkner to remain at home until he finished his novel. Then, they promised, he would return to Hollywood to fulfill the remainder of his obligation. Additionally, Random House agreed to pay him an advance of $500 a month so he could work on the novel relieved of financial constraints.

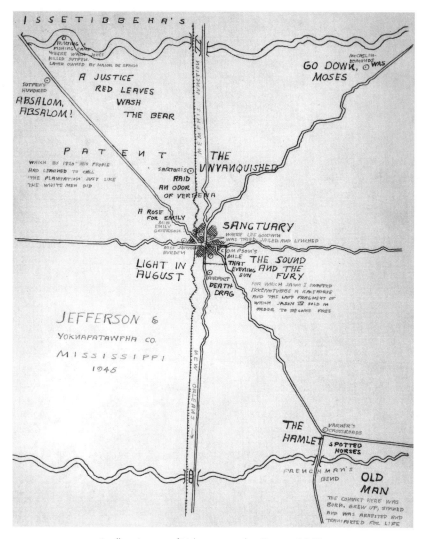

Faulkner's map of Yoknapatawpha County, 1945.

A major turning point in Faulkner's career came in April 1946, with the appearance of Malcolm Cowley's edition of *The Portable Faulkner*, published by Viking Press. Cowley, one of the country's leading critics and the literary editor of the *New Republic*, had long admired Faulkner's work and was perplexed that all but one of Faulkner's previous books were out of print. Aware of Faulkner's growing reputation in France, Cowley wanted to bring Faulkner to the attention of a wider reading public in the United States. With

Faulkner's approval and assistance, Cowley put together a representative collection of what he called Faulkner's "Yoknapatawpha Saga."

To supplement Cowley's selection of short stories and novel excerpts, Faulkner wrote an "Appendix" to *The Sound and the Fury* and supplied an updated map of his Yoknapatawpha County. Cowley added an influential introduction that interpreted Faulkner's novels and stories as a huge mosaic presenting a "legend of the South" that extends from the displacement of Native Americans by white settlers to the mid-years of the twentieth century. "All the separate works are like blocks of marble from the same quarry," Cowley wrote. "They show the veins and faults of the mother rock."

The Portable Faulkner could not have come at a better time for Faulkner. Still not free of his "enslavement" to Warner Bros.; still in debt with only the dole from Random House as support; and worried about Warner's claim to the rights of whatever he wrote, Faulkner was deeply discouraged and in danger once more of lapsing into depression and heavy drinking.

Ironically, about this time Faulkner won a $250 prize for a story Ober had submitted to an *Ellery Queen Mystery Magazine* contest. Faulkner wrote to Ober: "What a commentary. In France I am the father of a literary movement. In Europe I am considered the best modern American and among the first of all writers. In America, I eke out a hack's motion picture wages by winning second prize in a manufactured mystery story contest."

But *The Portable Faulkner* was about to change that situation. Caroline Gordon's favorable review of the book appeared on the front page of the *New York Times Book Review*, and Robert Penn Warren added his high praise in his review essay in the *Atlantic*. Warren disagreed with Cowley, however, in one important respect: Faulkner's work, Warren explained, is much more than a "legend of the South"; it dramatizes "our general plight and problem." This distinction fueled a debate that continues even today: to what degree is Faulkner a "southern" writer, and to what degree does he use southern materials as a means to express broader, even universal concerns? Interestingly, Faulkner agreed with Warren on this point: as he wrote to Cowley during the production of the *Portable*, "I'm inclined to think that my material, the South, is not very important to me. I just happen to know it, and don't have time in one life to

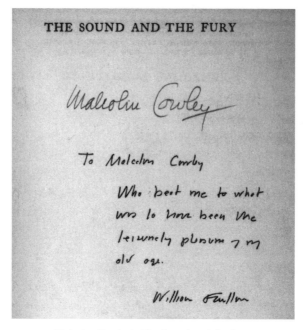

Malcolm Cowley's *The Sound and the Fury*,
inscribed by Faulkner.

learn another one and write at the same time." But most critics and readers have continued to follow Cowley's lead in viewing Faulkner as primarily a "southern" writer.

A little-discussed, but extremely important, result of the publication of *The Portable Faulkner* was that college professors now had a handy anthology of Faulkner's writings to use as a text in their classrooms. Because of the difficulty of his texts, Faulkner has never been popular with general readers; a large percentage of the sales of his books has come from students being required to purchase the books for their college literature classes. And it was *The Portable Faulkner* that initiated this trend.

The appearance of *The Portable Faulkner* also served to induce Random House to issue a joint Modern Library edition of *The Sound and the Fury* and *As I Lay Dying*. This little book also became a popular textbook and provided a whole generation of Faulkner readers their introduction to the great author.

Naturally, Faulkner was elated over the wide acceptance of Cowley's Yoknapatawpha edition. Faulkner often said that his last book would be a "Doomsday Book, the Golden Book, of Yoknapatawpha County," and now Cowley had done that for him. Faulkner expressed his appreciation in the inscription he wrote in Cowley's copy of *The Sound and the Fury* (which Faulkner had borrowed for the writing of his "Appendix," since he couldn't locate a personal copy of the book): "To Malcolm Cowley who beat me to what was to have been the leisurely pleasure of my old age."

In the spring of 1947 Faulkner became involved in an unfortunate situation that put him at odds with one of his principal rivals as America's greatest modern novelist, Ernest Hemingway. Faulkner agreed to visit some English classes at Ole Miss, with the understanding that no notes would be taken and nothing published of what he said. In one of those sessions he was asked to rank the best of the contemporary writers. He did so, listing them in this order: Thomas Wolfe, Faulkner, John Dos Passos, Hemingway, and John Steinbeck. He explained Hemingway's lower ranking by saying that Hemingway had "no courage," since he always stuck with the simple style he had mastered and would not risk experimenting with other forms.

Unfortunately, contrary to the agreement Faulkner had with the university, a student took notes on Faulkner's comments, and a school official arranged to have them published. When Hemingway discovered that he had been accused of having no courage, he was furious. He asked a friend, Brigadier General "Buck" Latham, to write to Faulkner, describing Hemingway's heroism under fire as a war correspondent attached to Latham's unit.

Embarrassed by the whole affair, Faulkner answered Latham's letter, explaining that he knew of Hemingway's wartime record but that his reference was to Hemingway the writer, not the man. He enclosed a note of apology for Latham to pass on to Hemingway. But the damage had been done. As was the case earlier with Sherwood Anderson, Faulkner found himself estranged from a fellow writer.

Faulkner was now approaching his fiftieth birthday. He continued to work on his fable, but with mixed success. Even though Warner Bros. had agreed to extend his leave until he finished the book, he made little progress. He could not settle on the order of the narrative, and he rewrote and rewrote many scenes. Using a tactic he had learned in story conferences in Hollywood, he penned an outline of the plot on the wall of his office at Rowan Oak, but still the writing stalled. Sometimes he suffered from writer's block and could not write at all. This was a new experience for him. "I don't write as fast as I used to," Faulkner wrote to Ober.

With the fable seemingly coming to a dead end, Faulkner tried another tack. He remembered a story idea he had considered several years earlier: "a mystery story, original in that the solver is a negro, himself in jail for the murder and is about to be lynched, solves murder in self defense." Perhaps because he had returned to his familiar locale of Yoknapatawpha, Faulkner found that the writing came quickly on this new novel. He completed the manuscript in a little over three months. The story of how a young boy, his black playmate, and an old woman assist Lucas Beauchamp in proving his innocence, the novel was published on September 27, 1948, as *Intruder in the Dust*. It was his first novel in six years; and while a slight book compared to his masterpieces, it would nevertheless bring him great benefits.

For one thing, as Faulkner noted, what started out to be a short "whodunit" had "jumped the traces" to become a commentary on current race relations in the South, with the thesis "that the white people in the south, before the North or the govt. or anyone else, owe and must pay a responsibility to the Negro." The gradual bonding of a young white boy, Chick Mallison, and an African American, Lucas Beauchamp, somewhat reminiscent of the relationship of Huck and Jim in Twain's *Adventures of Huckleberry Finn*, struck a sensitive chord for readers at the dawn of the civil rights movement. Using Gavin Stevens as a spokesperson for gradualism, Faulkner examined both the southern and northern views of integration—which, incidentally, were coming into play as a significant issue in the 1948 presidential election. Expressing views that Faulkner would offer himself in later political essays, Stevens argues against forced federal intervention but implores southerners to extend justice to their black fellow citizens. In tracing Chick Mallison's progress from viewing Lucas Beauchamp as a stereotypical Negro to seeing him as a fellow human being, Faulkner maps the journey that he hopes other white southerners will be willing to travel in the days to come. It was his own personal journey as well.

Partly because of the national concern that was developing over race issues, *Intruder in the Dust* received a great deal of media

Sailing on Sardis Lake.

Sailing on Sardis Lake, 1950s.

attention. Reviewers found that the book not only demonstrated considerable artistic merit but also made a significant social and political statement. Edmund Wilson of the *New Yorker*, who titled his review "William Faulkner's Reply to the Civil-Rights Program," felt that the novel represented "a new note to come from the South," "something more than Faulkner's own courageous and generous spirit, some new stirring of public conscience." Another reviewer thought

Lucas Beauchamp was "one of the most convincing Negro characters in American fiction."

The national attention given the novel translated into sales. The first printing of the novel sold more than 15,000 copies, Faulkner's best numbers since *Sanctuary*. Additionally, MGM paid $50,000 for the film rights to the book, $40,000 of which went to Faulkner. For the first time in years, Faulkner was solvent. He bought a better car, a garden tractor, and a new roof for Rowan Oak. He bought a sailboat for use on Sardis Lake. He also rewarded himself with a trip to New York, his first in nine years.

In New York Faulkner made the rounds with all the Random House editors—Bennett Cerf, Robert Haas, and Saxe Commins. He renewed acquaintances with Jim Devine, his friend from his Greenwich Village days in the 1920s, and with Hal Smith, who had published *The Sound and the Fury*. He attended parties and went to dinners with actress Ruth Ford, with whom he had become close friends in Hollywood. He met Malcolm Cowley for the first time.

But the endless round of parties and receptions, all involving heavy drinking, proved too much for Faulkner's fragile health. One day, after he failed to answer his phone in the Algonquin Hotel, friends found him drunk and only semiconscious in his room. They quickly called an ambulance and arranged to have him checked him into a nearby sanitarium. After only one night, however, Faulkner refused to stay there, despite the doctor's insistence that he needed several days of treatment.

Malcolm and Muriel Cowley came to the rescue, agreeing to take Faulkner home with them to their Connecticut farm and supervising his recuperation. While there Faulkner, once he had overcome the pangs of withdrawal, engaged in friendly conversations with Cowley; and Cowley took Faulkner for a long drive through the New England countryside. During the visit Faulkner inscribed several of his books to Cowley, though in an unsteady hand that evidenced his sick condition.

After a few days Faulkner was well enough to travel back to New York and from there on to Mississippi. Before he left for home, he had a dozen roses delivered to Muriel Cowley.

In Oxford, Faulkner resumed work on the Christ fable, but still the novel stalled. However, working on *Intruder in the Dust*, in which

Vicky Fielden and Jill Faulkner with Claude Jarman, Jr.,
actor in *Intruder in the Dust*, 1949.

Gavin Stevens is a major character, had perhaps suggested another project to Faulkner's mind: a collection of detective stories featuring Stevens. A few of these stories had already appeared in magazines, Faulkner reminded Random House, and he could add a concluding story bringing Stevens's story up to date. The process was similar to the manner in which he had created *The Unvanquished*, *The Hamlet*, and *Go Down, Moses*. Random House liked the idea, hoping to capitalize on the momentum created by *Intruder in the Dust*, and the collection of Stevens stories, titled *Knight's Gambit*, appeared on November 7, 1949.

The principal Faulkner event that year, however, was the MGM filming of *Intruder in the Dust* on location in Oxford. The writer once known as "Count No 'Count" was now responsible for bringing Hollywood to Oxford. Forty of the town's merchants placed a full-page notice in the *Oxford Eagle* celebrating the event, and a number of local citizens were given parts in the movie. Some citizens, though, were not pleased that the story of an attempted lynching would be filmed in their hometown.

Faulkner himself had ambivalent feelings about the movie. He resented the hullabaloo of the town's excitement, but he cooperated fully with director Clarence Brown, driving around the county with him to scout out locations for filming and utilizing his screenwriting experience to read over the final script and offer suggested revisions. He even took his mother and Jill to view some of the filming, and he and Estelle hosted a cast party at Rowan Oak. Faulkner especially liked Brown, a fellow southerner, who impressed Faulkner as someone who would honestly treat the race issue without portraying Mississippians with ridicule and scorn.

The world premiere of the showing of *Intruder in the Dust* was held at the Lyric Theatre in Oxford on October 11, 1949. Faulkner attended the event, though reluctantly, and only at the persuasion of his family, including Aunt 'Bama from Memphis. She sent a message that she would be attending the premiere, wearing her best dress, and she expected her grand-nephew to escort her to the event. Faulkner complied.

The movie version of *Intruder in the Dust* proved to be a great success, not only in Oxford but also around the country. Interest in Faulkner was growing rapidly. *Life* magazine planned an elaborate feature on his life and his work. Carvel Collins of Harvard and John Pilkington of the University of Mississippi were preparing to offer Faulkner seminars at their respective universities, and two other Ole Miss professors, Harry Campbell and Ruel Foster, were writing the first book-length critical study of Faulkner's novels. Random House was planning to issue *The Collected Stories of William Faulkner*. Yoknapatawpha was now on the American map as well as that of Mississippi.

But none of this attention, public and critical, relieved the great unhappiness in Faulkner's personal life. His relationship with Estelle was in shambles; his Hollywood lover Meta had remarried Wolfgang Rebner; his drinking bouts were becoming more frequent and lasting longer; and he was suffering from severe depression. What saved him from total despair, at least for the time being, was a friendship he developed with a young, aspiring writer, Joan Williams.

Faulkner first met Joan, a twenty-year-old student who lived in Memphis, in August 1949 when a relative of hers drove her to Rowan Oak to introduce her to the famous writer. Faulkner was immediately attracted to the beautiful young woman, and he agreed to advise her on her writing. Over the next several months they corresponded, and occasionally met, sometimes in Oxford, sometimes in Holly Springs or Memphis—even in New York City and at Bard College, where Joan became a student and, after graduation, a staff member. Faulkner's interest in Joan quickly turned romantic, but Joan resisted his seductive advances, preferring instead to know him as a surrogate father and a mentor.

Perhaps as an excuse so they could be together more often, Faulkner proposed that he and Joan collaborate on writing projects. One typescript that Faulkner forwarded to his agent, a short play entitled "Innocent's Return," carried the names of both Faulkner and Joan on the title page, although Williams later could not recall doing any writing on it. From time to time Faulkner sent Williams pages from the draft of another play, *Requiem for a Nun*, with invitations for her to read them and make suggestions or even revisions; but again, there is no evidence that Williams ever did any writing on that project either.

One of Faulkner's letters to Joan from this period clearly reveals the midlife crisis he was experiencing, as well as his hope that Joan could somehow help him escape it. Knowing her, he wrote, reminded him of "something remembered out of youth: smell, scent, a flower, not in a garden but in the woods maybe, stumbled on by chance, with no past and no particular odor and already doomed for the first frost: until 30 years later a soiled battered bloke aged 50 years smells or remembers it, and at once he is 21 again and brave and clean and durable." Once again Faulkner, like the narrator of his early poems, had discovered a young nymph that he identified with an ideal love and happiness. Once again he was destined to be disappointed.

TEN

The Nobel Prize

ON DECEMBER 10, 1950, FAULKNER WAS AWARDED THE NOBEL Prize for Literature in ceremonies held in Stockholm, Sweden. Understandably, this event brought significant changes to Faulkner's life and career. The privacy that he had so long cherished and fought to preserve was shattered irrevocably. He was now a citizen of the world.

This conflict between the private and public Faulkner is evidenced in his attitude toward the prize and even in his delivery of the acceptance speech. He initially refused to attend the ceremony, but under pressure from family, Random House, and even the U.S. ambassador to Sweden, he finally relented to go. But in Stockholm he was nervous and withdrawn, clearly uncomfortable with the whole proceedings. Only the presence of Jill, who had accompanied him, and the discovery of a new and sympathetic friend, a Swedish woman named Else Jonsson, made the trip at all bearable.

His speech ranks as the best ever given by an American laureate and one of the best of all twentieth-century American speeches. Using the occasion to address "the young men and women ... among whom is already that one who will some day stand here where I am standing," he spoke of the importance of writing about "the problems of the human heart in conflict with itself which alone can make good writing." He linked the writer's voice to humankind's "inexhaustible voice" and expressed his faith in immortality: "I believe that man will not merely endure: he will prevail." He concluded: "The poet's, the writer's, duty is to write about these things. It is his privilege to help man endure by lifting his heart, by reminding him of the courage

Faulkner receiving the Nobel Prize, 1950.

Faulkner and Jill at the Nobel Prize ceremony, 1950.

Faulkner at the Nobel Prize ceremony, 1950.

and honor and hope and pride and compassion and pity and sacrifice which have been the glory of his past. The poet's voice need not
merely be the record of man, it can be one of the props, the pillars to
help him endure and prevail."

Ironically, few people heard Faulkner's inspiring words. He spoke
in a soft voice and stood too far away from the microphone. "We did
not know what he said until the next morning," said one member of
the audience. It was as if Faulkner, though thrust onto the world's
stage, was still trying to retreat into his personal privacy. That contra-
diction would continue for the rest of his life.

Back home in Oxford, Faulkner decided to use some of the
$30,000 Nobel Prize money to help his neighbors. "I want to give
some money to the poor folks of Lafayette County," he told his
Uncle John. He contributed to a scholarship fund for a local African
American educator. He paid to have a drainage ditch widened and

Faulkner with Jill and classmates, 1951.

improved to assist area farmers. He created a music scholarship at the University of Mississippi in honor of Dorothy Commins.

The following spring Faulkner would be called upon to give another speech, one much closer to home. Jill was being graduated from high school, and her classmates had persuaded her to secure her father as a commencement speaker. Speaking to an audience numbering more than a thousand, Faulkner encouraged the students to strive "to change the world for man's peace and security." They must undertake this challenge individually, Faulkner advised, since "It is not men in the mass who can and will save Man. It is Man himself . . .—Man, the individual, men and women, who will refuse always to be tricked or frightened or bribed into surrendering, not just the right but the duty too, to choose between justice and injustice, courage and cowardice, sacrifice and greed, pity and self. . . ." He concluded by encouraging the students to "Never be afraid to raise your voice for honesty and truth and compassion, against injustice and lying and greed."

The speech took less than five minutes, and some in the audience had not been able to hear his soft-spoken words; but the occasion

Bird hunting with Jill, 1950s.

Faulkner, 1950s.

was a great success. Faulkner was no longer Count No 'Count in Oxford, and he had made his daughter extremely proud.

In the weeks and months to come, Faulkner continued his pursuit for the love of Joan Williams, who was still elusive and reluctant. They corresponded frequently, as he continued to advise her on her writing, and he visited her on the campus of Bard College in Annandale-on-Hudson, New York, and in New York City. Estelle knew of the relationship, and she was very unhappy about the situation; but by now she and Faulkner had settled into what today would be called "an open marriage." As long as Faulkner kept his affairs far removed from Oxford, Estelle would grant him his freedom.

By now Faulkner had developed grave doubts about being able to make a successful play of *Requiem for a Nun*. However, as he so frequently did, he found a way to recycle and rework the material into another format. Employing the technique that he identified as "counterpoint," he wrote three prose narratives—"The Jail," "The Courthouse," and "The Golden Dome"—about the history of Yoknapatawpha County and Mississippi, interspersing them among the acts of the play that treated the life of Temple Drake eight years after the events in *Sanctuary*. Thus Temple's attempt to find redemption from the suffering and guilt associated with her life in Memphis is placed within the context of the larger pattern of human experience—or, as Faulkner expressed it, "the vast weight of man's incredible and enduring *Was*"— as represented in the Yoknapatawpha chronicle. In this regard *Requiem for a Nun* may be usefully compared to John Milton's *Paradise Lost*, as both narratives reiterate the biblical story of a loss of Edenic innocence, subsequent guilt and retribution, and a hoped-for redemption.

Rowan Oak.

Faulkner and Mrs. Faulkner at Rowan Oak, 1950s.

Even after *Requiem for a Nun* was published on September 27, 1951, Faulkner, for the sake of his friend Ruth Ford, to whom he had promised the stage role of Temple, continued to work on the play version. He made two trips to Cambridge, Massachusetts, where rehearsals were being conducted, to meet with Albert Marre, whom Ruth had enlisted to direct the play. Later Marre traveled to Oxford to continue his discussions with Faulkner. But the revisions they worked out satisfied neither, and soon Faulkner dropped out of the project. He assigned the rights to the play to Ford who, along with her husband, Zachary Scott, gallantly continued efforts to salvage the play. Eventually there would be a play version of *Requiem for a Nun*, but it would take Ruth and Scott several years to accomplish this.

In July 1952, with no play or book in progress, suffering from back pain, still unhappy in his personal life and marriage, and with Joan continuing to reject his amorous advances, Faulkner fell into the depths of despair. He often did this between books, drowning his pain and unhappiness in alcohol, but this time the situation seemed worse. He wrote to Saxe Commins: "For the first time in my life, I am completely bored, fed up, my days are being wasted. . . . I think now I may, to save my soul, something of peace, contentment, save the work at least, quit the whole thing, give it all to them, leave and be done with it. . . . Then maybe I will get to work again, and get well again. But I don't have enough time left to spend it like this."

When the situation worsened, with Faulkner's drinking spinning more and more out of control, Estelle summoned Commins to travel to Oxford to assist. It was Commins's first visit to Oxford, and he described what he found in a letter to his Random House colleagues: "The fact is that Bill has deteriorated shockingly both in body and mind. He can neither take care of himself in the most elementary way or think with any coherence at all. This may be only evidence of his condition in a state of acute alcoholism. But I believe it goes much deeper and is real disintegration." Commins continued: "What to do? I realized at once that this is a case for professional care. No good intentions or friendship or understanding of the psychological causes are of any help at this stage. He needs a hospital, nurses, discipline."

Commins persuaded Faulkner that he needed professional care, and Faulkner allowed himself to be transported to Gartly-Ramsay Hospital, a psychiatric care facility in Memphis. He stayed there a week, undergoing diagnosis and treatment, but he refused an extended stay.

In November Faulkner's health rallied sufficiently to enable him to participate in the filming of a documentary about his life and career, produced on location in Oxford for the television show *Omnibus*. In the film he moves about Oxford and Greenfield Farm, interacting with friends, neighbors, and tenants. This short movie, *William Faulkner of Oxford*, represents one of only three instances in which Faulkner is captured in moving film footage.

Faulkner, 1950s.

Phil Stone and Faulkner, 1952.

Faulkner with producers of TV documentary, 1952.

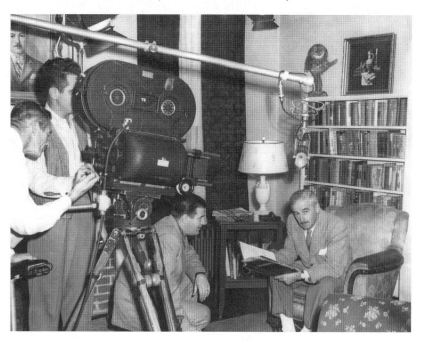

Faulkner during filming of *William Faulkner of Oxford*, 1952.

Faulkner with hunting buddies, 1952.

When the depression returned, Faulkner concluded that he needed time away from Oxford and arranged a six-month residence in New York. Commins and his Random House partners supported the move, feeling that they could better monitor Faulkner's condition and more easily arrange necessary treatment if he were closer to them. For a brief while the strategy worked. Faulkner used an office at Random House when he felt like writing, he saw Joan Williams from time to time, and he frequently visited with Saxe and Dorothy Commins in their home in Princeton.

All too soon, however, the double demons of depression and drink seized him again, the result being that he spent much of his time in New York in doctors' offices and hospitals or under home care. One psychiatrist who examined Faulkner during this period concluded that he was "a man built to suffer." The reason, the doctor surmised, was that Faulkner desperately craved affection but, perhaps because of his many unhappy relationships from childhood onward, feared that he would never find it.

Saxe Commins in his office at Random House, c. 1954.

For too long Faulkner's work on *A Fable* had languished. Even a trip to Paris to re-familiarize himself with the French setting had failed to reignite the project. But now, under Commins's sympathetic care and direction, Faulkner found the resolve to resume writing on the "big book." As he moved toward the completion of the novel, his confidence in the book returned. He wrote to Meta Rebner: "Am just finishing what I think is the best work of my life and maybe of my time." Once again Faulkner was discovering, and demonstrating to others, that, for him, the only successful anodyne to pain and suffering was artistic creation. Only the writing, his way of "saying No to death," gave his life meaning and purpose. As he had frequently stated, his religion, his immortality, was his art.

In November 1953 Faulkner and Commins worked together, several days and nights in Commins's Princeton home, giving the chapters of *A Fable* their final design and order. They scattered the pages of the manuscript about the room—on the desk, on chairs, on the bed, on the floor—and discussed the most effective order of the narrative.

Faulkner at Hadrian's Tomb, Rome, 1954.

They settled, as Faulkner typically did, on a disrupted chronology, opening the story at midpoint of the corporal's final week and then ranging back and forth among the other days, thereby creating delayed revelations and suspense.

The novel had been ten years in the making, and it had become a labor of love for Commins, as for Faulkner. And only the two of them could fully realize the terrible anguish and travail that had gone into its creation. Whatever readers and critics would think of the book, it would stand as a heroic triumph of achievement over despair and potential failure.

Faulkner interrupted his final editing of *A Fable* in late November 1953 when his old Hollywood friend, Howard Hawks, requested his assistance on *Land of the Pharaohs*, an epic movie Hawks planned to shoot on location in Egypt. Faulkner met Hawks in Paris, and then the film crew traveled to Stresa, Italy; St. Moritz, Switzerland; and Rome before heading on to Cairo for the actual filming. Faulkner was assigned to work with veteran screenwriter Harry Kurnitz on

Jean Stein.

the script. Their collaboration resulted in a very mediocre movie, but it did produce one of the legendary stories of Faulkner's film career. As they worked on the script, Kurnitz confessed to Faulkner that he had no idea how pharaohs should speak. It was mutually agreed that they would be made to sound like Confederate generals.

While working on *Land of the Pharaohs* Faulkner met Jean Stein. Only nineteen years old, the socialite daughter of the founder of the Music Corporation of America, Jean was infatuated with Faulkner upon their first meeting; and Faulkner, who had just learned that Joan Williams was planning to marry Ezra Bowen, turned to Jean as a substitute. "A queer thing has happened to me," Faulkner wrote to Saxe Commins, "almost a repetition; this one is even named Jean. . . . She came to me in St Moritz almost exactly as Joan did in Oxford." Jean would join Faulkner in Cairo and see him often in the United States in the months and years to come.

A Fable was published on August 2, 1954, and the *Newsweek* issue of the same date carried Faulkner's photograph on the cover. Although the book was awarded a Pulitzer Prize, it was summarily dismissed by both readers and critics. Set in France during World War I and thus not a part of the Yoknapatawpha series, limited in originality by its heavy dependence on the New Testament story of Christ, and murky and seemingly contradictory in its intent, the novel puzzled reviewers, who called it a "calamity" and a "failure." Even Faulkner ultimately seemed displeased with it.

Yet *A Fable* represents one of Faulkner's most serious and profound commentaries on life in the modern world. It is a war novel, depicting a mutiny led by a French soldier and his dozen followers; but in the final analysis it is about much more than war. The generals and their war machinery represent all the bureaucratic and tyrannical forces that would enslave humans and rob them of their individuality and personhood. The French corporal, the Christ figure of the novel, represents human freedom, personal dignity, and brotherhood. The generals seem all-powerful, but Faulkner seems to be saying that as

Celebrating Jill's wedding, 1954.

long as there are heroic, uncompromising individuals like the corporal and his disciple, the runner, humanity is not irrevocably lost or doomed. The setting of the novel is France, not Mississippi, but the familiar struggle to "endure and prevail" is the same theme found in Faulkner's Yoknapatawpha fiction. It was also a pattern Faulkner had just demonstrated in his personal life by bringing his ten-year struggle with *A Fable* to completion.

Faulkner dedicated *A Fable* to Jill, who was approaching her twenty-first birthday. Later he explained, "It was just a way of saying, 'Goodbye to your childhood, you are grown now and you are on your own.'" That sentiment proved prophetic. A month later, in St. Peter's Episcopal Church in Oxford, Faulkner gave his daughter's hand in marriage to Paul Summers, a lawyer living in Charlottesville, Virginia.

ELEVEN

Ambassador and Statesman

FAULKNER WAS NEVER AT EASE IN HIS ROLE AS A PUBLIC FIG-
ure, but during the later years of his life he accepted the role with considerable dignity and grace. He did so in large part because he held
strong convictions, more and more so with the passing years, about
some of the major issues of the day. Race relations, as so many of his
novels and stories reveal, had long been a serious concern of his; but
following the U.S. Supreme Court's desegregation decision in 1954,
the problem became more acute. Fiercely patriotic, Faulkner also felt
obligated to defend the United States in its Cold War conflict with
the Soviet Union. Additionally, personal liberty and privacy, lifelong
concerns, were, he felt, becoming increasingly threatened in a bureaucratic society based on commercialism and greed. Faulkner addressed
these issues in various ways.

In August 1954 Faulkner traveled to São Paulo, Brazil, to attend
a six-day International Writers' Conference—the first of several
overseas trips he would make in coming years as a cultural ambassador on behalf of the United States government. On the trip to and
from São Paulo he made brief stopovers in Lima, Peru, and Caracas,
Venezuela. In each city he held press conferences, attended dinners
and receptions in his honor, and, as he explained in his follow-up
report, sought "to help give people of other countries a truer idea
than they sometimes have of what the U.S. actually is." The South
American trip was so successful and personally rewarding that
Faulkner asked the State Department to consider him for further
ambassadorial assignments.

Wednesday

Dear Phil:

I haven't seen the LIFE thing yet, and wont. I have found that my mother is furious over it, seems to consider it inferentially lies , cancelled her subscription.

I tried for years to prevent it, refused always, asked them to let me alone. It's too bad the individual in this country has no protection from journalism, I suppose they call it. But apparently he hasn't. There seems to be in this the same spirit which permits strangers to drive into my yard and pick up books or pipes I left in the chair where I had been sitting, as souvenirs.

What a commentary. Sweden gave me the Nobel Prize. France gave me the Legion d'Honneur. All my native land did fro me was to invade my privacy over my protest and my plea. No wonder people in the rest of the world dont like us, since we seem to have neither taste nor courtesy, and know and believe in nothing but money and it doesn't much matter how you get it.

Yours,

Bill

This time I wasn't even consulted, didn't even know it was being done, nor did my mother. She knew she was being photographed and specifically asked the photographer not to print the picture anywhere.

This seems to me to be a pretty sorry return for a man who has only tried to be an artist and bring what honor that implies to the land of his birth.

Faulkner letter to Phil Mullen, 1953.

In July 1955 Faulkner ventured into the arena of public opinion with an essay in *Harper's*, titled "On Privacy." The essay evolved from his failed attempt to prevent *Life* magazine from publishing a story on his personal and private life, which he wished to maintain as both personal and private. Faulkner explained his position by stating his belief that "only a writer's works were in the public domain," that "until the writer committed a crime or ran for public office, his private life was his own." In Faulkner's view, all three of the principals—he, the reporter assigned to do the story, and the publisher—were victims of a commercialism run amuck, a demand for information, the more sensational the better, that would increase circulation of the magazine.

Faulkner in Japan, 1955.

Faulkner framed his objections within the context of his under-standing of the American Dream as created by the founders of the Republic—the right of every individual to be free from mass coer-cion and unwanted intrusion upon his private life. "Freedom of the Press," one of the bulwarks of American democracy, had been cor-rupted into the power of a wealthy institution to trample the rights of individuals. Along with his own personal experience, Faulkner cited Charles Lindbergh and Robert Oppenheimer as examples of individuals whose privacy had been destroyed by a tasteless, greedy press. "The point is that in America today any organization or group, simply by functioning under a phrase like Freedom of the Press or National Security or League Against Subversion, can postulate to it-self complete immunity to violate the individualness—the individual privacy lacking which he cannot be an individual and lacking which individuality he is not anything at all worth the having or keeping—of anyone who is not himself a member of some organization or group numerous enough or rich enough to frighten them off." This belief in individuality, in the individual's right to freedom and privacy, is the common thread that connects Faulkner's views on almost every topic, whether writing, politics, race, gender, or personal values.

Faulkner in Paris, 1955.

Faulkner in Manilla, 1955.

In August 1955 the State Department, endorsing Faulkner's offer to accept additional overseas assignments, sponsored a nineteen-day trip to Japan, where Faulkner visited Tokyo, Nagano, and Kyoto. At a press conference in Tokyo he talked about literature, racial problems in the United States, and East-West relationships. In Nagano he participated in a week-long seminar attended by more than fifty Japanese scholars and students, discussing with them a broad range of literary and cultural topics. In appreciation of Faulkner's visit, the Japanese participants presented him with a large scroll signed, with greetings, by all of the scholars. Today that scroll is on display in the Nagano public library as part of an exhibit that commemorates Faulkner's visit to the city. After concluding the seminar in Nagano, Faulkner traveled on to Kyoto for more press conferences and social activities. Then it was back to Tokyo for some final activities and the return trip home.

At the beginning of the Japanese visit Faulkner, extremely anxious and worried, had resorted to his usual method of handling crisis— heavy drinking. At that point Leon Picon, the U.S. embassy official who was assigned to oversee Faulkner's itinerary, feared that the entire agenda might have to be cancelled. But Faulkner pulled himself together, telling Picon, "I won't let you down. The U.S. government commissioned me to do a job and I'll do it." As the days passed Faulkner gained strength and confidence, and by the end of the trip he was interacting comfortably with reporters and others and showing marked improvement in his public speaking skills.

Closer to home was a larger concern than international relations. Confronted by the wave of hysteria and violence that followed in the wake of the Supreme Court's *Brown v. Board of Education* decision ordering the desegregation of southern schools, Faulkner sought to warn his fellow southerners of the mistake they were making. He wrote a series of letters that were published in the Memphis *Commercial Appeal*, imploring his fellow citizens to adapt to changing conditions and not try to refight the Civil War. He rebutted one letter writer who stereotyped African Americans who lived in the slums of Memphis as shiftless. He weighed in on the separate-but-equal policy that Mississippi was using to circumvent school integration. He wrote: "Our present schools are not even good enough for white folks. So what do we do? make them good enough, improve

Faulkner at horse farm in Italy, 1955.

Faulkner in Italy, 1955.

Faulkner at horse farm in Italy, 1955.

them to the best possible? No. We beat the bushes, rake and scrape to raise additional taxes to establish another system at best only equal to that one which is already not good enough, which therefore won't be good enough for Negroes either; we will have two identical systems neither of which are good enough for anybody."

In another letter he argued that the only dual school system Mississippians should be contemplating would be academic schools for all who qualify, black as well as white, and trade and craft schools, again irrespective of color, for those not competent for or interested in the academic schools. Faulkner ended this letter by describing himself as "an old veteran sixth-grader" who holds "no degrees nor diplomas from any school.""Maybe," he concluded, "that's why I have so much respect for education that I seem unable to sit quiet and watch it held subordinate in importance to an emotional state concerning the color of human skin."

On August 28, 1955, Emmett Till, a black teenager from Chicago visiting relatives in the Mississippi Delta, was kidnapped by two white men and horrifically murdered for allegedly whistling at the wife of one of the men. Faulkner, at the time on a stopover in Rome after his trip to Japan, was besieged by reporters asking for his comments on the crime. He subsequently prepared a 400-word statement that he released to the press. With words he had weighed carefully, Faulkner reminded his readers that the white race comprises only one-fourth of the world's population; therefore, crimes such as this one presented a threat to the survival of Mississippi, the United States of America, and indeed the entire white race. Faulkner called upon all Americans "to present to the world one homogenous and unbroken front, whether of white Americans or black ones or purple or blue or green." He concluded, in perhaps the strongest statement he ever made about racial injustice: "Because if we in America have reached that point in our desperate culture when we must murder children, no matter for what reason or what color, we don't deserve to survive, and probably won't."

Only a couple of months after the Emmett Till murder, Faulkner's good friend and neighbor, Jim Silver, a history professor at the University of Mississippi and an influential member of the Southern Historical Association, arranged for Faulkner to speak at the annual meeting of the association, to be held at the Peabody Hotel in Memphis. Silver, a political liberal, and other association officials were planning a program focusing on the impact of the Supreme Court's desegregation decision on southern life and institutions. In addition to Faulkner, Benjamin Mays, a noted African American educator and civil rights activist who was president of Morehouse College in Atlanta, and Cecil Sims, a noted lawyer, would be principal speakers.

Interestingly, in his remarks Faulkner placed his discussion of race and segregation within the context of the global threat of communism. He opened with the remark, "To live anywhere in the world of A.D. 1955 and be against equality because of race or color, is like living in Alaska and being against snow." But then he quickly moved to the imminent danger of communist domination around the world. In both Europe and Asia, Faulkner argued, only England was assured of not being communist within the next ten years. The reason communism had not prevailed thus far, Faulkner continued, was America, "not just because of our material power, but because of the idea of individual human freedom and liberty and equality on which our nation was founded." This belief that human beings can be free, Faulkner said, "is the strongest force on earth; all we need to do is, use it." However, that belief and the power it entails were being undermined and possibly defeated by the racial inequality evidenced throughout American history. Were it not for that shameful history, Faulkner said, "there would have been no Supreme Court decision about how we run our schools." It was time now for all Americans, of whatever color, to "confederate, and confederate fast," to grant to every American full political and economic freedom and equality.

Faulkner concluded: "We must be free not because we claim freedom, but because we practice it; our freedom must be buttressed by a homogeny equally and unchallengeably free . . . so that all the other inimical forces everywhere—systems political or religious or racial or national—will not just respect us because we practice freedom, they will fear us because we do."

Predictably, the public pronouncement of his views on race (liberal in his day, moderate in terms of later developments) made Faulkner something of a pariah in his hometown and native state. He received annoying and threatening phone calls. One correspondent called him "Weeping Willie Faulkner" and accused him of betraying his native land. Even his own family, especially his brother John, sided against him. One of his harshest critics was his longtime friend Phil Stone, who included the following comment in a letter to an acquaintance who had inquired if Stone would ask Faulkner a question about one of his books: "Since he has taken the position he has in turning his back on his own people and his native land, I don't care to ask him anything."

Actually, Faulkner had not turned his back on the South, as he made explicitly clear (too clear, as it turned out) in an interview he granted in 1956 to Russell Warren Howe, for publication in *The Reporter* and the London *Sunday Times*. Faulkner had been drinking heavily in the days leading up to the interview; as a result, he was not in the best physical or mental shape. As the interview progressed, Howe, a British reporter, pressed Faulkner to discuss the South's hard-line opposition to integration, and Faulkner, as he often did when outsiders criticized his native region, became defensive and militant. "As long as there's a middle road," Faulkner said, "I'll be on it. But if it came to fighting I'd fight for Mississippi against the United States even if it meant going out into the street and shooting Negroes." Further on, he reiterated the point: "I will go on saying that the Southerners are wrong and that their position is untenable, but if I have to make the same choice Robert E. Lee made then I'll make it."

Almost immediately, Faulkner realized he had overreached, exaggerating his position. While he was at heart (like Gavin Stevens in *Intruder in the Dust*) a believer in states' rights politics, he did not advocate violence in support of that position, and he certainly was no defender of the Lost Cause of the Confederacy. In the aftermath of the publication of his provocative remarks, he tried to distance himself from his statements, all but acknowledging that he was inebriated during the interview. "They are statements which *no sober man* [emphasis added] would make, nor, it seems to me, any sane man believe," he wrote in a clarifying statement. But the damage had been done, causing some liberals, and many African Americans, to question the sincerity of his commitment to civil rights.

In a further attempt to clarify and explain the remarks he made to Howe, Faulkner accepted the invitation of *Ebony* magazine, which catered to an African American audience, to submit an essay on race. Faulkner titled the piece "A Letter to the Leaders in the Negro Race"; *Ebony* published it as "If I Were a Negro." In the short essay Faulkner commended African American leaders and particularly the NAACP for their successful efforts in abolishing segregation. But now, Faulkner said, white southerners should be granted a little breathing room, time to reevaluate their historical stance on race and assimilate the radical changes that had been thrust upon them. "Go slow. . . . Be flexible," Faulkner counseled black leaders to say to their followers. "The watchword of our flexibility must be decency, quietness, courtesy, dignity; if violence and unreason come, it must not be from us." Citing Gandhi, Faulkner advocated a peaceful, patient activism that would ultimately win the day. Meanwhile,

Faulkner advised, blacks should be directed to concentrate on self-improvement: "We must learn to deserve equality so that we can hold and keep it after we get it."

As this essay makes abundantly clear, Faulkner was a gradualist in his approach to integration and civil rights, but the claim by James Baldwin, the noted African American author, that Faulkner's "Go slow" meant "Don't go" seems excessive and even unfair. Faulkner did sincerely desire to see the South change, but he believed that precipitous change effected by physical or psychological force would, in the long run, do more harm than good.

In 1956 Faulkner accepted the invitation of President Dwight D. Eisenhower to serve as chairman of the Writers' Committee for the People-to-People Program, an organization designed to identify ways to foster better relations between Americans and citizens of other countries. A number of prominent writers declined to become involved in the endeavor, and some expressed surprise that Faulkner was willing to do so. But as he explained to a friend, "When your President asks you to do something, you do it."

Over the next few weeks, with the assistance of Harvey Breit, a literary critic who agreed to serve as Faulkner's co-chair, as well as Saxe Commins and Jean Ennis of Random House, who offered to help with the correspondence and paperwork, Faulkner sent out questionnaires to other authors, asking for their suggestions on how to improve international relations. Once the results had been received and tabulated, a meeting was held in New York to finalize committee recommendations. The final report, signed by Faulkner, John Steinbeck, and Donald Hall, recommended that visa requirements be eased to enable refugees from Hungary and other countries to travel to the United States; that people from across the globe be brought to America for two years to experience a "normal American life"; and that the U.S. government develop a program to distribute American books, plays, and movies to foreign countries. As an addendum, the committee asked that Ezra Pound be freed from incarceration. That plea carried a reference to Faulkner: "While the Chairman of this Committee, appointed by the President, was awarded a prize for literature by the Swedish Government and was given a decoration by the French Government, the American Government locks up one of its best poets."

Faulkner at Random House, New York, c. 1957.

Faulkner with Victoria and Bill Fielden, 1950s.

Even as circumstances and his own strongly held convictions and sense of patriotic duty pushed him more and more into the public arena, Faulkner still found time for his fiction. At this stage of his life new ideas for stories were hard to come by, but there were previous stories and characters that needed advancement, and there were gaps in his history of Yoknapatawpha still to be filled. Ever since Malcolm Cowley had identified an overall plot and design in Faulkner's corpus, Faulkner had seemed desirous of fleshing out the whole, tying up the loose ends and supplying the missing pieces. There was a good deal of this type of work to be done.

Principal among such tasks was the completion of the story of the Snopeses, begun way back in 1926 with *Father Abraham* and continued with *The Hamlet* and numerous short stories, but still unfinished. In December 1955 Faulkner picked up the story of Flem Snopes again, drawing upon previously published short stories and adding new material that describes Flem's climb in Jefferson after he had conquered Frenchman's Bend. Set against Flem are "Snopes watchers" Gavin Stevens, a Heidelberg-educated lawyer who is futilely in love with Eula Snopes, and V. K. Ratliff, the sewing-machine salesman and man of the people whom Flem had bested in a business deal at the end of *The Hamlet*. But Stevens and Ratliff prove no match for the shrewd and underhanded Flem. A mixture of tall-tale yarnspinning and social realism, *The Town* would be dedicated to Phil Stone, "who did half the laughing for thirty years."

During this period Faulkner continued to see Jean Stein from time to time—in Mississippi and New York—and he collaborated with her on what most critics feel is the finest interview Faulkner ever granted. Published in the prestigious *Paris Review*, the interview contains some of Faulkner's most revealing statements about his art. "A writer needs 3 things:" Faulkner said, "experience, observation, imagination, any two of which, at times any one of which, can supply the lack of the others." All art, Faulkner stated, attempts "to arrest motion, which is life, by artificial means and hold it fixed so that 100 years later when a stranger looks at it, it moves again since it is life." Concerning the writer's duty, Faulkner claimed: "The writer's only responsibility is to his art. . . . If a writer has to rob his mother, he will not hesitate; the *Ode on a Grecian Urn* is worth any number of old ladies." With regard to his Yoknapatawpha series, he commented, "I like to think of the world I created as being a kind of keystone in the Universe; that, as small as that keystone is, if it were ever taken away, the universe itself would collapse."

Like Joan Williams before her, Jean Stein was becoming increasingly concerned about Faulkner's age and, more worrisome, his excessive drinking and poor health. She turned from him, just as Joan had done, to a younger man. Faulkner, once again, was heartbroken.

Ironically, just as Faulkner and Jean were breaking up, Estelle, after all her years of humiliation and unhappiness, offered Faulkner a divorce. Jill, Cho-Cho, and Malcolm were all grown up and married, so there seemed little left to hold her marriage together. She was now willing to give Faulkner his freedom.

However, Faulkner declined her offer. He would live out his life married to the first woman he ever loved.

TWELVE

Last Years

IN APRIL 1956 FAULKNER ACCEPTED AN INVITATION TO BECOME writer-in-residence at the University of Virginia in Charlottesville, and he began his duties there in February 1957. A major incentive for the move was so that he and Estelle could be near Jill and her family, which now included the Faulkners' first grandson. But in his first press conference Faulkner gave an additional reason: "I like Virginia, and I like Virginians. Because Virginians are all snobs, and I like snobs. A snob has to spend so much time being a snob that he has little left to meddle with you, and so it's very pleasant here." Faulkner wasn't being altogether facetious. Here again was his expressed desire for privacy, and perhaps, too, he was glad to be temporarily removed from Oxford and the hostility he was feeling there as a result of his controversial stand on integration and race.

Jill located a house for her parents on Rugby Road, just a twenty-minute walk from the campus. Faulkner began his duties immediately, meeting with Professor Frederick Gwynn's American literature class and answering the students' questions about *The Sound and the Fury*, their current assignment. Gwynn, his colleague Joseph Blotner, and Floyd Stovall, chair of the department, comprised the committee that would oversee Faulkner's activities for the university. Both Gwynn and Blotner had served in World War II, Gwynn as a bomber pilot and Blotner as a bombardier, and Faulkner quickly bonded with both men. Gwynn's office became "the Squadron Room," where the three men would gather to drink coffee and swap stories. Later in the relationship Faulkner produced an illustrated citation for the

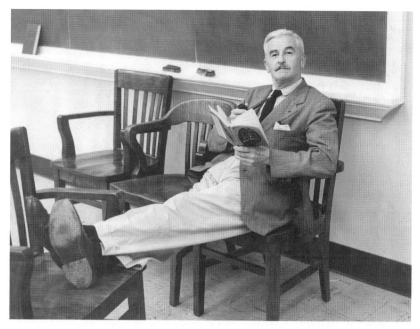

"Professor" Faulkner, 1957.

Faulkner with Professors Joseph Blotner and Frederick Gwynn, 1957.

Faulkner and Grover Vandevender, 1958.

Squadron, listing Gwynn as officer in charge of coffee, Blotner as officer in charge of cups, and himself as "chief ace and Jacdan [Jack Daniel's] liaison." Faulkner signed the citation as "E. V. Trueblood," using for the adjutant's name the occasional pseudonym he had first employed three decades earlier.

Throughout the remainder of the semester Faulkner met with classes, both undergraduate and graduate, as well as with other organizations and groups, both on campus and off. He also held conferences with individual students in the small office provided him. Gwynn persuaded Faulkner to allow the class and group sessions to be audio recorded, and the book that Gwynn and Blotner subsequently produced from the transcriptions of those tapes (*Faulkner in the University*) has become a valuable tool to Faulkner scholars and readers.

Among the real delights Faulkner found in Charlottesville were more opportunities to ride and hunt. Although Faulkner had been a dues-paying member of a hunt club in Germantown, just outside Memphis, for a number of years, he seldom participated in its hunts.

Faulkner in Greece, 1957.

Jill, continuing the love of horses and hounds she had learned from her father, was a member of the Farmington Hunt Club, eventually becoming its Master of Hounds. She introduced her father to Grover Vandevender, the huntsman of the club, and Faulkner became a frequent visitor to Vandevender's farm to practice his horsemanship. Faulkner never became an expert rider, but by autumn he would be good enough to join the other hunters in the annual fox hunt.

In March 1957, heeding the call of the State Department once again, Faulkner traveled to Greece for a two-week visit. While there he attended a stage performance of *Requiem for a Nun* and met the actor and actress who played the roles of Temple Drake and Gavin Stevens. He gave a speech to 1,200 members of the Workers Clubs of Athens and met with student groups. He traveled through the countryside to Delhi and Mycenae and aboard a yacht to Naupflion and other sites. Back in Athens, he was awarded the Silver Medal by the Athens Academy. In his acceptance speech Faulkner spoke as an American as well as a writer. "When the sun of Pericles cast the shadow of civilized man around the earth," Faulkner stated, "that shadow curved until it touched America." He said he would remind everyone in his home country "that the qualities in the Greek race—toughness, bravery, independence and pride—are too valuable to lose."

Returning to Charlottesville, Faulkner finished out the semester and awaited the publication of *The Town*, the second volume of the Snopes trilogy, which appeared on May 1. In it three narrators— V. K. Ratliff, Gavin Stevens, and Chick Mallison—tell how Flem Snopes, by now a figure of legend, moves from Frenchman's Bend to Jefferson, becomes superintendent of the town's water plant, and quickly conspires to become president of a bank, trading upon his wife's affair with the current president, Manfred de Spain, to advance his plan. Ratliff, Flem's nemesis from *The Hamlet*, enlists Stevens, a lawyer, as his partner in the fight against "Snopesism." Gavin is also in love with Eula Snopes but loses out to De Spain for her affection. Neither are Ratliff and Gavin successful in their opposition to Flem, who has invited more Snopeses to join him in Jefferson, the result being that the whole town is now overrun by the aggressive, amoral clan. At the end of the novel De Spain, publically exposed and scandalized, is hounded out of town, Flem becomes the bank president, and Eula commits suicide. Flem's avarice has now devoured Jefferson just as it had earlier devoured Frenchman's Bend.

Many readers found *The Town* quite entertaining and humorous, but most reviewers panned the novel. Alfred Kazin, a noted critic, described the novel as "tired, drummed-up, boring, often merely frivolous." Faulkner had never cared much for reviewers, and at this point of his life, the Nobel Prize, a Pulitzer Prize, the National Book Award, and other prestigious honors in hand, he could afford to care even less. Besides, he was already at work on his next book, the final volume of the Snopes saga, *The Mansion*.

For the last five years of his life Faulkner and Estelle shuttled back and forth between Charlottesville and Oxford. He still owned Greenfield Farm, and though the management of it was now largely left to his tenants, Faulkner felt obligated to put in an appearance there from time to time. Additionally, his mother was in failing health, and she required his help with doctors and medical expenses.

But he was rather enjoying his experience in Virginia and accepted an invitation to return a second year as writer-in-residence and then, after that, as the Balch Lecturer in American Literature. The high

At the University of Virginia, 1958.

Faulkner, University of Virginia, 1958.

Ruth Ford.

school dropout was now a faculty member of one of the oldest and most prestigious universities in the country. Not long afterward, to show his appreciation to the university, he added a codicil to his will, creating the William Faulkner Foundation which, among other things, would bequeath to the University of Virginia all of the manuscripts remaining in his possession.

One event in January 1959 that particularly delighted Faulkner was the New York opening of the play version of *Requiem for a Nun*. Faulkner had lost interest in the play after he successfully converted it into a novel in 1951, but, as an act of friendship, he had gladly assigned the rights to the play to Ruth Ford. Now, these several years later, Ruth and her husband, Zachary Scott, had succeeded in bringing the play to the stage. It had opened in London to positive reviews, with Ruth receiving extremely high praise for her role as Temple Drake. Now it was moving to New York. Faulkner could not attend the New York premiere, but he wrote to Ruth, congratulating her and adding, "God bless you. I only wish this play could be what you deserve." Unfortunately, the New York critics were not as impressed as the London ones, and the play closed after forty-three performances.

The Mansion, the third and final volume of the Snopes series, was published on November 13, 1959. This novel brings to a conclusion the rise and fall of Flem Snopes. Having climbed to the top of the money heap in Jefferson, Flem concludes that he is lacking in only one thing: respectability. And he intends to have it. While much of the content of the novel repeats material from *The Hamlet* and *The Town*, Faulkner fills out the trilogy with the murder of Flem by his cousin, Mink Snopes, who blames Flem for his twenty-year incarceration in prison for an earlier murder, and the story of Linda Snopes, Eula's daughter, whom Gavin Stevens has aided in escaping from her father's pernicious influence. Much like the escape of Caddy's daughter, Quentin, from Jason Compson's hatred in *The Sound and the Fury*, Linda's salvation adds a positive denouement to an otherwise tragic plot. And the treatment of Mink Snopes, despite his being a double murderer, reprises Faulkner's lifelong sympathy for the poor and downtrodden people of the earth.

Early reviewers, citing the excessive use of repetition from the earlier books, thought *The Mansion* to be the weakest of the Snopes novels, as it probably is, judged as a separate work. But in Faulkner's mind and imagination the Snopes narrative is all of one piece, not three novels but discrete chapters in one long chronicle; and in 1964 Random House honored Faulkner's intent by issuing a boxed set of the three novels under the title *Snopes: A Trilogy*. By then Warren Beck had become the first scholar to treat the Snopes trilogy as a unified whole, with his *Man in Motion: Faulkner's Trilogy*, published in 1961; and other critics, most notably James B. Watson and Joseph Urgo, have followed his lead. The result is that *Snopes* has risen steadily to a higher value in Faulkner's canon.

On October 16, 1960, Maud Falkner died. During her final illness Faulkner and Estelle were in Oxford, and Faulkner spent much of the time at her bedside. She had been the one person who had never faltered in her belief in him as a great writer, and now she would be gone. As she approached death Faulkner soothed her with stories of heaven. Listening to one of those stories, Maud asked, "Will I have to see your father there?" "No," Faulkner replied, "not if you don't want to." "That's good," his mother said. "I never did like him."

With the death of his mother, and his realization that Jill would never return to her birthplace to live, Faulkner's ties to Oxford were greatly diminished. He and Estelle would spend even more of their time in Virginia. But they continued to divide their time between Charlottesville and Oxford, partly to avoid having to pay taxes in Virginia as well as Mississippi.

In both places he continued with his riding, practicing his jumps in the pasture at Rowan Oak and riding with both the Farmington and Keswick clubs in Charlottesville. Eventually, however, Faulkner would pay a heavy price for his riding activities. Though he was not an expert rider, he was a high-risk one, relishing the dangers of the fast chase and the high jumps. He fell from his mounts on numerous occasions, incurring various types of injuries: broken ribs, a fractured collarbone, a concussion, cracked vertebrae, and broken teeth. Yet he refused to give up the sport.

Faulkner in paddock at Rowan Oak.

Practicing his jumps, c. 1960.

And, of course, he continued with his writing, working on what would become his final book, *The Reivers*. For the title he borrowed an archaic Scottish term for "robbers." The novel describes the serio-comic adventures of young Lucius Priest and his two adult sidekicks after they steal Grandfather Priest's automobile and journey to Memphis, where they consort with prostitutes and gamblers and Lucius learns some important lessons about responsibility and being a gentleman.

Faulkner, c. 1960.

Faulkner's estrangement from Oxford continued to deepen, partly because of what he learned that his friends and neighbors were doing back there. Phil Stone sold some of his Faulkner items to the University of Texas. Maud Brown sought Jim Silver's assistance in arranging for the publication of "The Wishing Tree," the story that Faulkner had given to her dying daughter years before. John Cullen, a hunting companion, published a book of his recollections of Faulkner. All such actions Faulkner viewed as invasions of his privacy and, more importantly, betrayals of friendship.

By now Faulkner and Estelle had purchased a home in Charlottesville, but their hearts were set on something else. They had fallen in love with Red Acres, a 250-acre estate, with a hundred-year-old brick house and a panoramic view of the Blue Ridge Mountains. Faulkner began to explore financial arrangements that would enable him to acquire the property.

Despite his increasingly bad health in his last years, Faulkner continued to accept occasional invitations for public appearances. He conducted a writer's seminar at Princeton University, fulfilling a promise he had made to Saxe Commins before Commins's death. He spoke at a UNESCO meeting in Denver. By popular request of the host nation, he made a two-week trip as a cultural ambassador to Caracas, Venezuela, to participate in a U.S.-sponsored program on international relations. He traveled to New York to present a Gold Medal for Fiction to John Dos Passos and then again to receive the same award from the National Institute of Arts and

Letters for himself. Faulkner's gold medal was presented to him by fellow Mississippi author Eudora Welty. At the same ceremony, Joan Williams was awarded a $10,000 prize for her novel, *The Morning and the Evening*, on which Faulkner had provided advice and assistance.

One trip, however, Faulkner declined to make. President John F. Kennedy invited him to the White House for a formal dinner. Faulkner refused to go, saying, "I'm too old at my age to travel that far to eat with strangers."

In April 1962 Faulkner paid a two-day visit to West Point Military Academy. Faulkner had always been enamored of the military life; additionally, his son-in-law, Paul Summers, who accompanied him on the visit, was a 1951 graduate of the academy. At West Point Faulkner attended a formal dinner hosted by the superintendent, General William C. Westmoreland, read a section of his forthcoming book to the cadets and guests, held a press conference, and visited a couple of classes. But as everyone noticed, especially toward the end of the visit, Faulkner looked extremely tired and worn out.

On June 4, 1962, just one month before his death, Faulkner's last book, *The Reivers*, was published. This novel has frequently been compared to Shakespeare's final play, *The Tempest*, in that it ends a writing career that has included dark tragedies with a happy, light-hearted comedy. In *The Reivers* Faulkner returns to the Memphis setting he had used in *Sanctuary*, but the book also represents something of a farewell tour of Yoknapatawpha, with numerous mentions of names and places made familiar in earlier novels and stories. Significantly, Faulkner dedicated the book to his grandchildren, gifting them with a benediction that life, despite its hardships and agony, is still worth living.

Faulkner and Estelle were back in Oxford by the time *The Reivers* came out, and Faulkner delivered an inscribed copy of the book to Phil Stone, even though the two men were hardly speaking at this point in their relationship. Depressed, and constantly hurting from his many injuries, Faulkner checked in with his doctors, and he shared with his nephew Jimmy his premonitions of his imminent death. Yet, recklessly, he continued to ride horses.

On Sunday, June 17, during a ride through Bailey's Woods, Faulkner was thrown from his horse and, once again, seriously injured. In the days following, to ease the pain, he started drinking heavily. As his condition worsened, Estelle and Jimmy decided that he needed to be taken to Byhalia for treatment; and Faulkner did not quarrel with the decision.

Jimmy and Estelle drove Faulkner to Wright's Sanitorium on the afternoon of July 5 and stayed with him until the nurses and doctor had checked him in and completed an examination. Then Jimmy and Estelle returned to Oxford. Before they left, Jimmy told Faulkner, "Brother Will, when you're ready to come home, let me know and I'll come for you." "Yes, Jim," Faulkner said, "I will."

Faulkner seemed to be resting comfortably as the night progressed, but shortly after midnight he awakened, sat up on the edge of his bed, and then, without a word, collapsed. Dr. Wright administered heart massage and attempted mouth-to-mouth resuscitation, but all efforts failed. Faulkner was dead of a heart attack. On July 6, 1962, at age sixty-four, on the Old Colonel's birthday, he passed through the "wall of oblivion" he had often talked about. What he had written a year earlier on the occasion of another great author's death now applied to himself as well: "When the door shut for him, he had already written on this side of it that which every artist who also carries through life with him that one same foreknowledge and hatred of death, is hoping to do: *I was here.*"

In 1954, in his "Foreword" to *The Faulkner Reader*, Faulkner had expressed his hope, like that of every writer, that his work might live on after his death. "Some day he will be no more, which will not matter then, because isolated and itself invulnerable in the cold print remains that which is capable of engendering still the old deathless excitement in hearts and glands whose owners and custodians are generations from even the air he breathed and anguished in; if it was capable once, he knows that it will be capable and potent still long after there remains of him only a dead and fading name."

Today, legions of Faulkner readers around the globe attest to the realization of that hope.

Afterword

———————————⚹———————————

SINCE HIS DEATH FAULKNER'S FAME AND INFLUENCE HAVE spread around the world. His works have now been translated into more than forty languages. Nobel laureates Gabriel García Márquez of Columbia, Kenzaburo Oe of Japan, Jorge Vargas Llosa of Peru, and Mo Yan of China, as well as a host of other international authors, have acknowledged Faulkner's influence upon their work. Faulkner can no longer be considered merely a "southern" writer, or even an "American" one. His appeal today is truly global.

Faulkner's growing reputation has spawned what is often referred to as "the Faulkner industry." Since his winning of the Nobel Prize in 1950, academics have published more than one hundred books and articles per year on Faulkner and his works. Four universities—Virginia, Mississippi, Texas, and Southeast Missouri—own major collections of his books, manuscripts, and papers; and several other schools and institutions hold smaller collections. The University of Mississippi has hosted an annual Faulkner and Yoknapatawpha Conference each year since 1974—the longest-running American conference devoted to a single author. A William Faulkner Society exists in both the United States and Japan. In 2006 Oprah Winfrey's Book Club, which has an estimated 600,000 members, read three Faulkner novels during Winfrey's "Summer of Faulkner." Seven of Faulkner's novels and seven of his short stories have been adapted into movies.

Faulkner's literary works are therefore well known by now. Perhaps less well known is the story of the man who wrote the books. A number of excellent Faulkner biographies have been published, but those are primarily written by academics for academics. This current book aims for a different, and wider, audience—general readers, and especially younger ones. Its purpose and hope are that its readers will come to a greater appreciation not only of the literary works by one of the world's great writers but also of the man, the artist, who created the works.

In his Nobel Prize acceptance speech Faulkner spoke of "the agony and sweat of the human spirit" that goes into artistic creation. For Faulkner, that struggle was especially acute. Poor and neglected for much of his life, suffering from chronic depression and the disease of alcoholism, unhappy in his personal life—Faulkner overcame tremendous obstacles to achieve his success. One of the major themes of his novels and stories is endurance, and his biography exhibits that same quality in abundance. Like the most admirable of his characters, Faulkner the man endured, and he ultimately prevailed. Not only his books, but also his life, can inspire others to do the same.

A Chronology of Faulkner's Life

1897	Born on September 25 in New Albany, Mississippi
1898	Family moved to Ripley, Mississippi
1902	Family moved to Oxford, Mississippi
1913	Drew a series of cartoons for a proposed Oxford Graded School yearbook
1914	Began friendship with Phil Stone
1915	Quit high school
1918	Jilted by childhood sweetheart, Estelle Oldham (who married Cornell Franklin); enlisted in the Canadian branch of the Royal Air Force; received pilot training in Toronto, Canada
1919	Enrolled as special student in University of Mississippi; first published in a national magazine (poem, "L'Apres-midi d'un Faune," in *New Republic*)
1921	Lived and worked briefly in New York; appointed post-master for University of Mississippi post office
1924	Published *The Marble Faun* (poems)
1925	Lived briefly in New Orleans; fell in love with Helen Baird; traveled in Europe
1926	Lived again in New Orleans; coauthored *Sherwood Anderson & Other Famous Creoles*; published first novel, *Soldiers' Pay*
1927	Published *Mosquitoes*

1929   Published first Yoknapatawpha novel, *Sartoris*; married Estelle Oldham; published *The Sound and the Fury*; worked in power plant on the Ole Miss campus

1930   Published *As I Lay Dying*; purchased Rowan Oak

1931   Daughter Alabama died, after living only nine days; published *Sanctuary* and *These 13* (short stories)

1932   Worked in Hollywood as screenwriter; father died; published *Light in August*

1933   Published *A Green Bough* (poems); received screen credit for coscripting *Today We Live*; *Sanctuary* filmed as *The Story of Temple Drake*; daughter Jill is born

1934   Published Doctor Martino and Other Stories

1935   Published *Pylon*; met Meta Carpenter while working in Hollywood

1936   Brother Dean killed in plane crash; coauthored screenplay, *The Road to Glory*; published *Absalom, Absalom!*

1938   Published *The Unvanquished*; bought Greenfield Farm

1939   Elected to the National Institute of Arts and Letters; published *The Wild Palms*

1940   Published *The Hamlet*

1942   Published *Go Down, Moses*; signed long-term screenwriting contract with Warner Bros.

1944   Coauthored screenplay, *To Have and Have Not*

1945   Walked out on Warner Bros. contract

1946   *The Portable Faulkner* published; received screen credit for *The Big Sleep*

1948   Published *Intruder in the Dust*; elected to American Academy of Arts and Sciences

1949   *Intruder in the Dust* filmed on site in Oxford; published *Knight's Gambit* (short stories)

1950   Awarded the Howells Medal for Fiction by the American Academy of Arts and Letters; published *Collected Stories*; received the 1949 Nobel Prize for Literature

1951   Won National Book Award for Fiction for *Collected Stories*; published *Requiem for a Nun*; delivered commencement address to daughter Jill's graduating class at University High School; named an Officer of the [French] Legion of Honor

1952   Delivered an address to the Delta Council, Cleveland, Mississippi

1953   Delivered commencement address to daughter Jill's graduating class at Pine Manor Junior College, Wellesley, Massachusetts

1954   Published *A Fable*

1955   Received National Book Award and Pulitzer Prize for *A Fable*; traveled to Japan for U. S. State Department; published *Big Woods*

1957   Became writer-in-residence at University of Virginia; traveled to Greece for State Department; published *The Town*; stage version of *Requiem for a Nun* presented in London

1958   Participated in Council on Humanities at Princeton University

1959   *Requiem for a Nun* presented on Broadway; published *The Mansion*

1960   Appointed to faculty at University of Virginia; mother died

1961   Traveled to Venezuela for State Department

1962   Received Gold Medal for Fiction from National Institute of Arts and Letters; presented reading at West Point Military Academy; published *The Reivers*; died of heart attack at Wright Sanitorium in Byhalia, Mississippi (July 6)

Works by Faulkner

1954   *The Faulkner Reader; A Fable; The Wild Palms and The Old Man*

1955   *New Orleans Sketches; Land of the Pharaohs; Big Woods*

1957   *The Town*

1958   *Three Famous Short Novels; New Orleans Sketches* (expanded edition)

1959   *Faulkner in the University; The Mansion*

1962   *Selected Short Stories of William Faulkner; The Reivers*

POSTHUMOUS PUBLICATIONS, WITH ORIGINAL DATE OF COMPOSITION

1977   *The Marionettes* (1920); *Mayday* (1926)

1979   *Mississippi Poems* (1924)

1981   *Helen: A Courtship* (1925)

1982   *Faulkner's MGM Screenplays* (1931–33)

1983   *Elmer* (1925); *Father Abraham* (1926–27)

1984   *Vision in Spring* (1921–23); *The De Gaulle Story* (1942)

1985   *Battle Cry* (1943)

1987   *Country Lawyer and Other Stories for the Screen* (1942–43)

1989   *Stallion Road* (1945)

Notes

PHOTOGRAPHS

I am extremely grateful to the institutions and individuals who cooperated and assisted in providing the photographs and illustrations included in this book. I am particularly indebted to Roxanne Dunn, head of the Special Collections at Southeast Missouri State University, and her assistant archivist, Tyson Koenig; Christopher Rieger, director of the Center for Faulkner Studies, Southeast Missouri State University; Lee Caplin, executor of the William Faulkner Literary Estate; Edward Gaynor, librarian for the Albert and Shirley Small Special Collections Library of the University of Virginia; Jessica Leming, Special Collections Librarian for the J. D. Williams Library at the University of Mississippi; and Leon C. Miller, head of the Louisiana Research Collection at Tulane University.

The Louis Daniel Brodsky Collection of William Faulkner Materials at Southeast Missouri State University contains one of the largest collections of Faulkner photographs in existence. The images on pages 4, 6, 7, 9, 15, 29, 30, 31, 36, 38, 40, 48, 49, 54, 55, 57, 64, 68, 69, 75, 77, 79, 82, 84, 85 (bottom), 88, 97 (bottom), 100, 103 (top), 106, 114, 121, 127, 130, 132, and 133 are reproduced courtesy of the Brodsky Collection.

The photographs on pages 12, 13, 14, 19, 22, 24 (top), 39, 45, 59, 61, 63, 65, 66, 83, 97 (top), 98, 99, 101 (bottom), 107, 108, 109, 113, and 116 are from the Joseph Blotner Archives, now part of the Brodsky Collection.

The photographs on pages 53, 91, 93, 101, 103 (bottom), 104, and 105 were made by Phil Mullen, longtime owner and editor of the *Oxford Eagle*. These photographs are provided courtesy of the Brodsky Collection.

The illustrations appearing on pages 20, 24 (bottom), 26, 27, 71, 86, and 112 are included courtesy of Lee Caplin, executor, William Faulkner Literary Estate.

The photographs on pages 125, 126, and 129 were made by Ralph Thompson and are used courtesy of Albert and Shirley Small Special Collections Library, University of Virginia.

The photographs on pages 25, 44, and 85 (top) are reproduced courtesy of Special Collections, J. D. Williams Library, University of Mississippi.

The photograph of Helen Baird on page 34 is provided courtesy of the William B. Wisdom collection of William Faulkner, Louisiana Research Collection, Tulane University.

ABBREVIATIONS USED IN NOTES

AA – *Absalom, Absalom!*
CS – *Collected Stories of William Faulkner*
ESPL – *Essays, Speeches, and Public Letters by William Faulkner*
FAB – *Faulkner: A Biography*
FCF – *The Faulkner-Cowley File*
FID – *Flags in the Dust*
FIU – *Faulkner in the University*
FOM – *The Falkners of Mississippi*
LIG – *Lion in the Garden*
M – *Mosquitoes*
MBB – *My Brother Bill*
NOS – *New Orleans Sketches*
Sanc – *Sanctuary*
Sar – *Sartoris*
SL – *Selected Letters of William Faulkner*
TU – *The Unvanquished*

PREFACE

xi   "It is my ambition": FCF, 126.
xi   "I am telling the same story": FCF, 14.
xi   "Any writer, to begin with": FIU, 103.

CHAPTER 1: ANCESTOR: THE OLD COLONEL

3   "I want to be a writer": FAB, 105.
10   "There Was a Queen": CS, 727.
11   "I never read any history": Robert Cantwell, "The Faulkners: Recollections of a Gifted Family," in *William Faulkner: Three Decades of Criticism*, ed. Frederick J. Hoffman and Olga W. Vickery (New York: Harcourt, Brace & World, 1963), 57.
11   "People at Ripley": Cantwell, 56.

CHAPTER 2: CHILDHOOD AND ADOLESCENCE

12   "They chop kindlin'": MBB, 11.
13   "one of those spells": SL, 20.

14 "We descended": FOM, 4.

14 "acorn baseball": MBB, 18.

16 "We were of a common conviction": FOM, 8.

16 "See that little boy": FAB, 16. Except when otherwise noted, all of the citations for Blotner's *Faulkner: A Biography* refer to the revised, 1984 edition.

16 "It was Mother": FOM, 17.

17 "the terror and grief": CS, 17.

17 "a tail-first inverted loop": FOM, 61.

17 "balloonitic": MBB, 110.

CHAPTER 3: YOUNG POET

23 "I gave him books to read": FAB (1974), 164.

23 "the medicinal value": LIG, 13.

27 "Those who can, do": TU, 262. Except when otherwise noted, quotations from Faulkner's novels are from the Vintage paperback editions.

29 "I reckon I'll be": FAB, 118.

CHAPTER 4: APPRENTICESHIP IN FICTION

32 "We'd walk and he'd talk": FIU, 21.

32 "You're a country boy": ESPL, 8.

33 "Where is that flesh": NOS, 12.

33 "I used to hear": FAB (1974), 406.

33 "WHATS THE MATTER": FAB, 135.

35 "stone lace": SL, 9.

36 "I have come to think": SL, 17.

36 "a genius who was electrocuted": FIU, 53.

36 "I have just written": SL, 17. Some critics think that this piece may have become the basis for the description of Temple Drake in the Luxembourg Gardens at the end of *Sanctuary*.

36 "saying No to time": *Elmer*, in *William Faulkner Manuscripts*, ed. Thomas L. McHaney and others (New York: Garland Publishing, Inc., 1987), 1:60.

37 "all those old coffee houses": SL, 29.

37 "Quietest most restful country": SL, 30.

37 "I waked up yesterday": SL, 31.

38 "An extraordinary performance": FAB, 181.

39 Faulkner's essay on Anderson: In the essay, which was published in the *Dallas Morning News* and reprinted in ESPL, 3-10, Faulkner acknowledges Anderson as a significant and influential writer, but he criticizes his overall production, calling him a "one-or-two-book man."

41   "Genius. A hard taskmaster" and following quotes: M (Dell paperback edition), 17, 149, 151, 152, 173, 187, 188, 205, 207, 208, 264, 265, 280, 280–81.

CHAPTER 5: CREATION OF YOKNAPATAWPHA

43   "that little patch up there": ESPL, 8. "Yoknapatawpha" is an old Indian word. A shortened version, "Yocona," still survives as the name of a north Mississippi river and a rural community near Oxford.

44   "I discovered that my own little": LIG, 255.

45   "a game outmoded and played": Sar, 380. The allusion is to the Battle of Roncevaux Pass, in the Pyrenees Mountains on the French and Spanish border, in 778, in which Roland, a commander in Charlemagne's army, was defeated and killed by the Basques. The story is told in *The Song of Roland*, one of the most famous works in French literature.

46   "Major Oldham's yard boy": FAB, 239.

46   "At last and certainly": SL, 38.

46   "The story really doesn't": FAB, 205.

46   "like a parent who is told": FAB, 206.

46   "I have a belly full": SL, 39.

46   "One day I seemed to shut": "An Introduction," *Southern Review* 8 (1972), 709; reprinted in *The Sound and the Fury: Norton Critical Edition*, 220. Faulkner probably found the story of the old Roman in Henryk Sienkiewicz's popular novel, *Quo Vadis*.

47   "heart's darling": FIU, 6.

48   *Sartoris/Flags in the Dust*: The original, longer version of the novel, with Faulkner's preferred title, would not be published until 1973.

49   "Read this, Bud": Ben Wasson, *Count No 'Count: Flashbacks to Faulkner* (Jackson: UP of Mississippi, 1983), 89.

50   "the most horrific tale": ESPL, 177.

50   "I want $500.00": FAB, 240.

51   "I would have been happy": FCF, 29.

51   "a kind of Battle Creek, Michigan": M, 264. Chooky Falkner once commented on the frequent complaint of Faulkner's neighbors that he often passed them on the street without speaking. Chooky noted that his uncle often treated him the same way, but added, "I always assumed he wasn't in Oxford then; he was in Jefferson."

CHAPTER 6: GENIUS UNLEASHED

52   "Faulkner when he wasn't": Stephen B. Oates, *William Faulkner: The Man and the Artist* (New York: Harper and Row, 1987), 87.

52   "I think that probably": A. I. Bezzerides, *William Faulkner: A Life on Paper*, ed. Ann Abadie (Jackson: University Press of Mississippi, 1980), 105.

53   "About 11 o'clock": Sanc (Modern Library edition), vii.

56   "Everybody in Oxford": FAB, 261.

56   Parallels between Faulkner and Flem Snopes: See, for example, Joseph Urgo, *Faulkner's Apocrypha: A Fable, Snopes, and the Spirit of Human Rebellion* (Jackson: University Press of Mississippi, 1989).

57   "Faulkner is the coming man": FAB, 263.

58   "Oh, Mr. Faulkner, do you write": FAB, 310.

59   "a man who outraged the land": SL, 79.

60   "rag-tag and bob-ends": AA, 303.

60   "story-teller's instinct": Harvey Breit, "Introduction," Modern Library edition of *Absalom, Absalom!*, v.

61   "those frantic little aeroplanes": FIU, 36.

61   "I'd got in trouble": FIU, 36.

62   "Dean was so badly disfigured": Oates, 134.

62   Faulkner's niece: Dean Faulkner Wells writes of her relationship to Faulkner in *Every Day by the Sun: A Memoir of the Faulkners of Mississippi* (New York: Crown Publishers, 2010).

63   "I could make him forget": FAB, 360.

64   "That's the girl": Wasson, 144.

64   "I think it's the best novel": Bezzerides, 83.

64   Faulkner and Random House: Random House had issued a signed, limited edition of *Idyll in the Desert* in 1931.

65   "I think we'd rather": FAB, 351, 371.

65   Nobel Prize winners: O'Neill won the 1936 Nobel Prize for Literature (awarded in 1937), Faulkner the 1949 Prize (awarded in 1950).

CHAPTER 7: FARMER

67   "Bill found more": MBB, 177.

67   "I'm not a literary man": Oates, 170.

68   "Some Cincinnatus of the cotton fields": FID (Vintage edition), 313–14.

68   "He said he had no feeling": MBB, 177.

69   "it was not the Negroes' fault": MBB, 195–96.

70   "contrapuntal": FIU, 171, 176.

72   "From her I learned": ESPL, 117–18.

73   *The Saturday Evening Post*: The *Post* typically paid Faulkner one thousand dollars for a story; the other periodicals paid from twenty-five dollars to five hundred dollars.

CHAPTER 8: GOLDEN LAND

74   "I have 60c in my pocket": SL, 154–55.

76   Faulkner's drafts of *The De Gaulle Story*: These and related materials, which total
      more than 1,000 pages and are now a part of the Brodsky Collection at Southeast
      Missouri State University, present the most comprehensive start-to-finish record
      of Faulkner's work on any single film project and offer compelling evidence that, at
      this stage of his Hollywood career, he was a skilled, professional screenwriter. See
      "Introduction," in Louis Daniel Brodsky and Robert W. Hamblin, eds., *A Compre-
      hensive Guide to the Brodsky Collection*, vol. 3: *The De Gaulle Story*, ix–xxxiii.

76   *The De Gaulle Story*: In November 1990, an adaptation of Faulkner's script titled *Moi,
      General DeGaulle* was shown on French television as part of the celebration of De
      Gaulle's one hundredth birthday and the fiftieth anniversary of the beginning of De
      Gaulle's resistance movement from London. See Robert W. Hamblin, "The Curious
      Case of Faulkner's 'The De Gaulle Story,'" *Faulkner Journal* 16 (2000–2001): 79–86.

76   "Let's dispense with General De Gaulle": Louis Daniel Brodsky and Robert W.
      Hamblin, eds., *Faulkner: A Comprehensive Guide to the Brodsky Collection*, 5 vols.
      (Jackson: University Press of Mississippi, 1982–1988), 3:395–96.

78   "I am writing a big picture": SL, 173–74.

78   "[Hawks] is going to establish": SL, 177.

79   "schmucks with typewriters": Bill Davidson, *The Real and the Unreal* (New York:
      Harper's, 1961), 242.

79   "Southern rectitude": Meta Carpenter Wilde and Orin Borsten, *A Loving Gentle-
      man: The Love Story of William Faulkner and Meta Carpenter* (New York: Simon
      and Schuster, 1976), 279.

79   Movie version of *To Have and Have Not*: See Bruce Kawin's introduction to his
      edition of *To Have and Have Not* (Madison: University of Wisconsin Press, 1980).

81   *Stallion Road*: See William Faulkner, *Stallion Road: A Screenplay*, ed. Louis Daniel
      Brodsky and Robert W. Hamblin (Jackson: University Press of Mississippi, 1989).

82   Hays Code censors: Named after William H. Hays, the president of the Motion
      Pictures Producers and Distributors of America, the Hays Code was implemented
      to screen and, if necessary, censor screenplays in accordance with generally accepted
      standards of morality and decency.

82   "Kindly keep down": Qtd. in "Introduction," Faulkner, *Stallion Road*, xv.

82   "a little strong for then": Qtd. in Louis Daniel Brodsky, "Glimpses of William
      Faulkner: An Interview with Stephen Longstreet," in Faulkner, *Stallion Road*, xxvi.
      Longstreet continues: "It was quite powerful, didn't pay too much attention to my
      novel. What Bill had done was to write a purely Faulknerian narrative, a beaut, all
      shadow and highlights and with the smell of the best horses."

83   "I'll never get it written": Wilde and Borsten, 309.

83   "It's my horse": FAB, 469.

CHAPTER 9: RETURN TO YOKNAPATAWPHA

84 "I feel that I have made a bust": SL, 204.

87 "All the separate works": Malcolm Cowley, ed., *The Portable Faulkner* (New York: Viking Press, 1946), 8.

87 "What a commentary": SL, 217–18.

87 "I'm inclined to think": SL, 185.

89 "Doomsday Book, the Golden Book": LIG, 255.

89 Cowley's copy of *The Sound and the Fury*: This book is now a part of the Brodsky Collection, Center for Faulkner Studies, Southeast Missouri State University.

90 "I don't write as fast": SL, 246.

90 "a mystery story": SL, 128.

90 "jumped the traces": SL, 262, 266.

91 "a new note to come": *New Yorker*, October 23, 1948: 120–28; reprinted in Nicholas Fargnoli, ed., *William Faulkner: A Literary Companion* (New York: Pegasus Books, 2008), 504.

92 "one of the most convincing": Horace Gregory, *New York Herald-Tribune Weekly Book Review*, September 26, 1948: 3; reprinted in Fargnoli, 470.

95 "of something remembered": FAB, 507.

CHAPTER 10: THE NOBEL PRIZE

96 Nobel Prize for Literature: Faulkner is frequently identified as the winner of the 1950 Nobel Prize, but such is not the case. In actuality he was the recipient of the 1949 prize, awarded a year late, during the same ceremony in which Bertrand Russell received the 1950 Nobel Prize for Literature.

96 Else Jonsson: Else was the widow of Thorsten Jonsson, a Swedish journalist who had been a great admirer of Faulkner. Though after Stockholm they met again only once, on Faulkner's visit to Paris in 1951, Else and Faulkner corresponded for the remainder of Faulkner's life.

96 Faulkner's Nobel Prize speech: One survey ranks Faulkner's speech at number thirty-three among famous twentieth-century speeches: http://www.american rhetoric.com/top100speechesall.html.

98 "the young men and women": ESPL, 119–20.

98 "We did not know": FAB, 533.

98 "I want to give some money": FAB, 535.

99 "It is not men in the mass": ESPL, 123–24.

100 "counterpoint": FIU, 122.

100 "The vast weight of man's": RFN, 215.

102 "For the first time in my life": Brodsky and Hamblin, 2:80.

102 "What to do": Brodsky and Hamblin, 2:91.

103   *William Faulkner of Oxford*: The others are some short excerpts from the Nobel Prize ceremony and the documentary *Impressions of Japan*, filmed during his 1955 visit to Japan.

105   "a man built to suffer": FAB, 568.

106   "Am just finishing what I think": Wilde and Borsten, 327.

106   "saying No to death": The best expression of this idea is found in Faulkner's "Foreword" to *The Faulkner Reader* (New York: Random House, 1954). The essay is reprinted in *Essays, Speeches, and Public Letters*, 179–82.

108   pharaohs and Confederate generals: Thomas A. Dardis, *Some Time in the Sun: The Hollywood Years of F. Scott Fitzgerald, William Faulkner, Nathanael West, Aldous Huxley, and James Agee* (New York: Scribner, 1976), 149.

108   "A queer thing has happened": Brodsky and Hamblin, 2:138.

108   Faulkner on *A Fable*: FAB, 588.

110   "It was just a way of saying": LIG, 162.

CHAPTER II: AMBASSADOR AND STATESMAN

111   "to help give people of other countries": FAB, 590.

112   "only a writer's works": ESPL, 66.

113   "The point is that in America today": ESPL, 70.

115   "I won't let you down": FAB, 602.

115   "Our present schools are not": ESPL, 216.

116   "an old veteran sixth-grader": ESPL, 219.

117   "to present to the world": ESPL, 223. Faulkner's statement was published in the September 9, 1955, issue of the *New York Herald Tribune*.

117   Southern Historical Association address: ESPL, 146–51. Faulkner expanded his remarks at the Southern Historical Association in an essay titled "On Fear: Deep South in Labor: Mississippi," published in the June 1956 issue of *Harper's*.

118   "Since he has taken the position": Brodsky and Hamblin, 2:220.

119   "As long as there's a middle road": LIG, 261–62.

119   "They are statements which no sober man": ESPL, 225.

119   "A Letter to the Leaders in the Negro Race": ESPL, 107–12.

120   Faulkner's "Go slow": James Baldwin, "Faulkner and Desegregation," *Nobody Knows My Name* (New York: Dell Publishing Co., 1961), 100.

120   "When your President asks you": FAB, 627.

120   "normal American life": Brodsky and Hamblin, 5:354–55. Pound had been convicted of treason against the United States for his pro-Fascist activities during World War II. Instead of being sent to prison, he was placed in a mental asylum.

122   *Paris Review* interview: LIG, 237–55.

122   "it moves again since it is life": Critics have noted in Faulkner's works the frequent use of art surrogates that demonstrate this principle—such as the commissary

ledgers in *Go Down, Moses* and the signature scratched on a windowpane in *Requiem for a Nun*.

CHAPTER 12: LAST YEARS

124   "I like Virginia": FAB, 633.

127   "When the sun of Pericles": ESPL, 152.

128   "tired, drummed-up, boring": *New York Times Book Review*, May 5, 1957, qtd. in FAB, 641.

130   "God bless you": FAB, 661.

131   Snopes trilogy: See James G. Watson, *The Snopes Dilemma: Faulkner's Trilogy* (Coral Gables, FL: University of Miami Press, 1972), and Joseph R. Urgo, *Faulkner's Apocrypha: A Fable, Snopes, and the Spirit of Human Rebellion* (Jackson: University Press of Mississippi, 1989).

131   "Will I have to see your father": FAB, 679.

134   "I'm too old at my age": FAB, 703.

135   "Brother Will, when you're ready": FAB, 713.

135   "wall of oblivion": FIU, 61.

135   "When the door shut": ESPL, 114.

135   "Some day he will be": ESPL, 182.

AFTERWORD

136   Faulkner's works adapted for movies: *Sanctuary, Intruder in the Dust, The Sound and the Fury, Pylon, The Hamlet, The Reivers, As I Lay Dying,* "Turn About," "Barn Burning," "A Rose for Emily," "Tomorrow," "The Bear," "Two Soldiers," and "The Leg."

A Selected Bibliography

Atkinson, Ted. Faulkner and the Great Depression: Aesthetics, Ideology, and Cultural Politics. Athens: University of Georgia Press, 2005.

Backman, Melvin. Faulkner: The Major Years: A Critical Study. Bloomington: Indiana University Press, 1966.

Bezzerides, A. I. William Faulkner: A Life on Paper. Ed. Ann Abadie. Jackson: University Press of Mississippi, 1980.

Blotner, Joseph. Faulkner: A Biography. New York: Random House, 1974. Rev. ed., 1984.

Brodsky, Louis Daniel, and Robert W. Hamblin, eds. Faulkner: A Comprehensive Guide to the Brodsky Collection. 5 vols. Jackson: University Press of Mississippi, 1982–1988.

Brooks, Cleanth. Faulkner: The Yoknapatawpha Country. New Haven, CT: Yale University Press, 1963.

Brown, Calvin S. A Glossary of Faulkner's South. New Haven, CT: Yale University Press, 1976.

Carothers, James B. William Faulkner's Short Stories. Ann Arbor, MI: UMI Research Press, 1985.

Cofield, Jack. William Faulkner: The Cofield Collection. Oxford, MS: Yoknapatawpha Press, 1978.

Cowley, Malcolm. The Faulkner-Cowley File: Letters and Memories, 1944–1962. New York: Viking Press, 1966.

Dain, Martin J. Faulkner's World: The Photographs of Martin J. Dain. Ed. Thomas S. Rankin. Jackson: University Press of Mississippi, 1997.

Doyle, Don H. Faulkner's County: The Historical Roots of Yoknapatawpha. Chapel Hill: University of North Carolina Press, 2001.

Falkner, Murry C. The Falkners of Mississippi: A Memoir. Baton Rouge: Louisiana State University Press, 1967.

Fargnoli, Nicholas, ed. William Faulkner: A Literary Companion. New York: Pegasus Books, 2008.

Fargnoli, A. Nicholas, Michael Golay, and Robert W. Hamblin. *Critical Companion to William Faulkner*. New York: Facts on File, 2008.

Faulkner, Jim. *Across the Creek: Faulkner Family Stories*. Jackson: University Press of Mississippi, 1986.

Faulkner, John. *My Brother Bill: An Affectionate Reminiscence*. New York: Trident Press, 1963.

Gresset, Michel. *A Faulkner Chronology*. Jackson: University Press of Mississippi, 1985.

Gwynn, Frederick L., and Joseph Blotner, eds. *Faulkner in the University: Class Conferences at the University of Virginia, 1957–1958*. Charlottesville: University of Virginia Press, 1959.

Hamblin, Robert W., and Charles A. Peek, eds. *A William Faulkner Encyclopedia*. Westport, CT: Greenwood Press, 1999.

Inge, M. Thomas, ed. *Conversations with William Faulkner*. Jackson: University Press of Mississippi, 1999.

Kartiganer, Donald M. *The Fragile Thread: The Meaning of Form in Faulkner's Novels*. Amherst: University of Massachusetts Press, 1979.

LaLonde, Christopher A. *William Faulkner and the Rites of Passage*. Macon, GA: Mercer University Press, 1996.

Meriwether, James B., and Michael Millgate, eds. *Lion in the Garden: Interviews with William Faulkner, 1926–1962*. New York: Random House, 1968.

Minter, David. *William Faulkner: His Life and Work*. Baltimore, MD: Johns Hopkins University Press, 1980.

Oates, Stephen B. *William Faulkner: The Man and the Artist*. New York: Harper & Row, 1987.

Parini, Jay. One Matchless Time: A Life of William Faulkner. New York: HarperCollins, 2004.

Peek, Charles A., and Robert W. Hamblin, eds. *A Companion to Faulkner Studies*. Westport, CT: Greenwood Press, 2004.

Pilkington, John. *The Heart of Yoknapatawpha*. Jackson: University Press of Mississippi, 1981.

Polk, Noel. *Children of the Dark House: Text and Context in Faulkner*. Jackson: University Press of Mississippi, 1996.

Singal, Daniel J. *William Faulkner: The Making of a Modernist*. Chapel Hill: University of North Carolina Press, 1997.

Slatoff, Walter J. *Quest for Failure: A Study of William Faulkner*. Ithaca, NY: Cornell University Press, 1960.

Sundquist, Eric. *Faulkner: The House Divided*. Baltimore, MD: Johns Hopkins University Press, 1983.

Volpe, Edmund L. *A Reader's Guide to William Faulkner: The Novels*. San Jose, CA: Authors Choice Press, 2001.

———. A Reader's Guide to William Faulkner: The Short Stories. New York: Syracuse University Press, 2004.

Waggoner, Hyatt H. *William Faulkner: From Jefferson to the World.* Lexington: University of Kentucky Press, 1959.

Warren, Robert Penn, ed. *Faulkner: A Collection of Critical Essays.* Englewood Cliffs, NJ: Prentice Hall, 1966.

Wasson, Ben. *Count No 'Count: Flashbacks to Faulkner.* Jackson: University Press of Mississippi, 1983.

Webb, James W., and A. Wigfall Green, eds. *William Faulkner of Oxford.* Baton Rouge: Louisiana State University Press, 1965.

Weinstein, Philip. *Becoming Faulkner: The Art and Life of William Faulkner.* New York: Oxford University Press, 2010.

Welty, Eudora. *On Faulkner.* Afterword by Noel Polk. Jackson: University Press of Mississippi, 2003.

Wilde, Meta Carpenter, and Orin Borsten. *A Loving Gentleman: The Love Story of William Faulkner and Meta Carpenter.* New York: Simon & Schuster, 1976.

Williamson, Joel. *William Faulkner and Southern History.* New York: Oxford University Press, 1993.

Index

Bundren, Vardaman, 55
Burton, Richard, 63
Butler, Lelia Swift, 15, 16
Byhalia, Mississippi, 135

Cairo, Egypt, 107, 108
Cambridge, Massachusetts, 102
Campbell, Harry, 94
Cantwell, Robert, 70
Caracas, Venezuela, 111, 133
Carothers, Chess, 18
Carpenter, Meta, 63–64, 75–76, 79, 94,
    106
Casablanca, 80
Cather, Willa, 58
Cerf, Bennett, 65, 92
Chandler, Raymond, 80
Charlottesville, Virginia, 110, 124, 126, 128,
    131
Chatto and Windus, 56
Chicago, Illinois, 117
Christmas, Joe, 19, 58, 59
Churchill, Winston, 77
Cincinnatus, 68
civil rights, 91, 120
Civil War, 4, 6, 9, 16, 43, 45, 59, 60, 66, 115
Clarksdale, Mississippi, 29
Cold War, 111
College Hill Presbyterian Church, 50
Collins, Carvel, 94
Commercial Appeal, 115
Commins, Dorothy, 98, 105
Commins, Saxe, 65, 92, 102, 105, 106–7,
    108, 120, 133
communism, 118
Compson, Benjy, 47, 51
Compson, Caddy, 24, 47, 130
Compson, Jason, 47, 130
Compson, Quentin, 47, 60
Confederacy, 5, 21, 119
Connecticut, 92
Conrad, Joseph, 16, 37
Cooper, Gary, 57
counterpoint, 70, 100

Cowley, Malcolm, xi, 81, 86–89, 92, 122
Cowley, Muriel, 92
Crawford, Joan, 57
Cuba, 80
Cullen, John, 133

Dallas Morning News, 145
Dark House, 59
David, King, 60
De Gaulle, Charles, 76–78, 148
de Spain, Manfred, 128
Denver, Colorado, 133
detective stories, 60, 93
Devine, Jim, 92
Dickens, Charles, 16, 74
Dilsey, 47
Dolan, Matthew, 6
Dos Passos, John, 58, 89, 133
Dostoevsky, Fyodor, 51
Double Dealer, The, 33
Drake, Temple, 49–50, 100, 102, 127, 130, 145
Du Pre, Jenny, 45
Dumas, Alexander, 16

Ebony, 119
Edmonds, Zack, 72
Eisenhower, Dwight D., 120
Eliot, T. S., 22, 25
Ellery Queen Mystery Magazine, 87
Elnora, 10
Emeline, 5
England, 37, 118
Ennis, Jean, 120
Euripides, 51

Falkner, Caroline, 5
Falkner, Dean, 13, 18, 45–46, 58, 61, 62, 79
Falkner, Fanny Forrest, 6
Falkner, Frances, 6
Falkner, James, 5
Falkner, John Wesley Thompson, 13, 14, 16,
    18, 23, 45
Falkner, John Wesley Thompson, Jr.
    ("Uncle John"), 98